Brendon -

I hope you enjoy
this book -

Coach Michel —

Brandon –

I hope you enjoy
this book –

Coach Mitchell –

Can Of Corn

A Baseball Memoir

by

Peter Michel

Bloomington, IN Milton Keynes, UK

authorHOUSE®

AuthorHouse™
1663 Liberty Drive,
Suite 200
Bloomington, IN 47403
www.authorhouse.com
Phone: 1-800-839-8640

AuthorHouse™ UK Ltd.
500 Avebury Boulevard
Central Milton Keynes, MK9 2BE
www.authorhouse.co.uk
Phone: 08001974150

First published by AuthorHouse   8/24/2007

ISBN: 978-1-4343-0682-1 (sc)

Printed in the United States of America
Bloomington, Indiana

This book is printed on acid-free paper.

DEDICATION

To the women in my life:
Ruth, Beth, Amy, Meg, Jo and G.G.

TABLE OF CONTENTS

INTRODUCTION

Did you ever want to write a book? I'm sure you have heard someone say "I could write a book". Perhaps you've even uttered the phrase yourself. Well here goes.

I want this book to be an easy read and sincerely hope that the contents within will engender memories for all of those who are faithful to the American pastime. BASE BALL - this is the way it was spelled at its genesis.

This book is more than an account of one's personal experiences, but of life in general, having baseball as the glue to hold it together. I hope that you enjoy it and perhaps relate to the benefits derived from having a passion for something, as baseball was and continues to be for me.

Life was simpler and neater during my childhood. I thought the road to adulthood would be for the most part smooth with perhaps a few bumps along the way. As I look back, I feel I have become stronger. My fabric, although somewhat tattered and torn, is being woven tightly again as I live out my later years. Dealing with un-static experiences has helped me deal with life's changes.

Jim Turner, the one-time pitching coach of the New York Yankees, so aptly put it as he quoted from Heraclites, "The only permanent thing in life is change." He then added, "You can't win in the biggies without a change."

Incidentally, at the end of each chapter I have included a trivia question for you to answer. The answers are found at the end of the book!

CHAPTER 1
HUMBLE BEGINNINGS

My first recollection of the game of baseball began when I was around six year's old living in Richmond Hill, Queens, New York with my family. The Michel family consisted of my Dad, Mom and my kid brother, Tom. We did have a pet gold fish, but Tom took care of that by giving him what he thought was fish food only to find out that it was soap suds! It is noteworthy at this time to mention that my Mom was the most direct influence in my getting involved and eventually consumed with baseball. My Mom and Dad most of the time looked at life as the glass "half empty", mainly I guess owing to their own life experiences World War I, the Depression, and World War II. I was born in February 1939, so we were about to embark as a nation into yet another world conflict. In our family we always seemed to be in an "underdog" state of mind. I believe that baseball buoyed our spirits during my formative years, but I sincerely believe that the game of baseball, which was often characterized by former baseball commissioner Bart Giamatti as a game that was invented to break your heart, did just that.

To this day I continue to remind players that out of ten times at bat, if you hit safely three times you might be destined for the Hall of Fame, since .300 batting averages are becoming somewhat of a rarity nowadays. Of course, becoming a rabid fan of the Brooklyn Dodgers didn't help me deal easily with success or hope for that matter!

My beginnings, playing and experiencing social interaction, and just plain growing up, began when I was introduced to the "lead up" games of baseball on the streets and playgrounds of New York. Stoopball, stickball, slapball, punch-ball, "one-a-cat", "catcher flyer up", (catch a fly you are up), all played with a "spaldeen", a pink rubber ball which when it was new had a pink resin on it similar to, but not as tasty as the pink film on the bubblegum in a new pack of baseball cards. These games were played daily when time permitted on our streets, backyards, tenement walls, and our ball fields. In punch ball I was a 'two sewer' player. You played this game in the streets between man-hole covers, and I could punch the ball a distance of two sewers. Some guys could hit beyond three man-hole covers receiving a home run for their punching prowess. Sometimes while playing a stickball game in the street we had to stop our games to let the Aqueduct Racetrack traffic pass. Before we started up again we always turned over the racetrack tickets that were thrown out by the drivers hoping to perhaps find an unclaimed winning stub.

The first field I played on was all concrete with painted bases and the ubiquitous scoreboard painted on the ground near home plate. We used an edge of a stone to write in the score. Chalk was used for making hopscotch for the girls in our neighborhood. My dungarees and knees took a beating. I could handle the knees, but my Mom was not too sympathetic about the ripped pants.

The social interactions with the guys on the block were very rewarding. I was one of the younger guys and luckily had some ability to be asked to play with the teenagers in the neighborhood. When I was asked to participate in a game that counted, I had my first experience of 'butterflies' in my stomach. But I prevailed and I didn't embarass myself or hurt the outcome of the game - at least that is what I remember. The nearest grass field was at John Adams High School and I never had a chance to play on it, but I would go down during the summer and watch some semi-pro games.

My first recollection of going to a professional baseball game was when I was around seven years old. I went with my Mom and my Uncle Tom to Ebbets Field to see the Dodgers play. Right then and there I started to experience the familial interaction that presents itself between family members. If memory serves me right, Ed Head was pitching for the Dodgers and they were playing the Boston Braves (they might have been called the B's). We sat in dead center field in the upper deck, and I could look to my left and see Bedford Avenue behind the right field fence. Uncle Tom and Mom became involved with the game from the first pitch on. Hot dogs and Crackerjacks held most of my attention. I was also interested in what was happening outside the right field fence. The light poles on Bedford Avenue were high enough that if you "shinned" up the pole to the top you could see the game. So kids were taking turns going up and down the pole to catch at least a half inning. They didn't have much more time because a patrolman was continually monitoring this and asking them to get down. The kids however devised a plan and waited until the patrolman had to leave to patrol another area. This was quite an interesting sight. I continued to go to a few more games at Ebbets Field, having started now to get involved in the intricacies of the game.

It was February 1950 when the Michels' made the move to the suburbs. My parents had been talking about it all fall, but I was never worried about it because I was having a good time at P.S 108 and playing baseball. I remember not liking one thing about P.S.108. The educational thrust at that time was to try to change left-handed children to write right-handed. I was all left and trying to change me was not all right! As a retired educator I now see that some educational wisdom is not always well founded! The experience led me to feign illness a few times and hide under the kitchen sink as my Mom tried to pry me out and send me to school.

So during February of my sixth grade, we moved to the Incorporated Village of Massapequa Park, New York, not to be confused with the Town of Massapequa which, for some unknown reason, surrounded us like a circle of wagons in that the boundary lines encircled our quaint little village. Unbeknownst to me, this was the start of the "Levittown Legacy" with houses sprouting up all over Nassau County, Long Island and soon to follow continuing out east to Suffolk County. An average priced house was $9,000. It was a two bedroom cape with an attached garage on a 60' X 100' plot. We finally had a backyard which was to become a bone of contention in that my Dad wanted to grow grass and I wanted to make a small replica of Ebbets Field. As fate would have it, I moved to 64 Pacific Street with an awful sore throat and I was immediately plopped into bed. I remember lying there sick as a dog saying to myself, "What the heck am I doing here?" At that time I did not realize that this was to be a rite of passage in my life's odyssey. The sore throat lingered until the following week, despite the fact that a doctor did come to visit me (remember those days when doctors still made house calls?). I am sure you will agree that all the doctor had to do was to show up at your bedroom door and you immediately felt better without any need for medication. I wanted to get on my way having been in my new abode for almost a week now.

But the thought of a new school did loom over me, and I think I became one of the first kids to consider "home schooling" as I did not want to climb on that school bus. I did start out, but as I got closer to the bus stop I slowed down my pace and conveniently missed the bus! No one knew this because I hid behind Healy's hedges. Seeing the fumes of the bus in the distance I now had to consider my options. Do I go back home saying that the bus arrived earlier than expected? That wouldn't work because my Dad had already taken the Long Island Railroad to New York and my Mom did not drive. Option number two was to return home with another sore throat, but my Mom was an astute human being and the only sore part of my body would then be my backside. So I decided on the third option and began my walking trek to school which was in the southwest region of Massapequa. Remember, I lived in the Park and we were surrounded by Massapequa, which, as Jerry Seinfield so aptly states in his stand-up comedy routine, is an old Indian name for "by the mall".

I started my six-mile journey walking west along side the Long Island Railroad tracks on a road called Front Street. It was early morning when lo and behold I saw a yellow bus with the name Union Free School District #23 emblazoned on its side. It was coming right towards me! I certainly was not going to flag it down; however, the bus driver, upon seeing me (probably the only sixth grader in Massapequa not in school), stopped abruptly and opened the doors. This was my first meeting with someone I can say to this day changed my life. Here sat a woman bus driver (not the usual in those days) with a babushka (scarf) on her head saying in a very authoritative voice, "Where are you going?" I replied that I was going to school. She said, "Get into the bus, and I will take you there". This was one option I hadn't considered!! She introduced herself and reminded me that this could never happen again since she had another bus route and I was "cramping her style". Upon dropping me off, she said, "Good luck" and again I was looking at bus fumes as I stood in front of the Massapequa Avenue Elementary School. I foolishly stood there thinking she might walk me in and I must admit I was scared to death as I approached the entrance. I was met by a man at the door who introduced himself as Mr. Lockhardt and he firmly shook my hand. He was the District Principal, equivalent in those days to the Superintendent of Schools.

What a beginning and I will state here and now, that I entered Mrs. Murray's sixth grade class never knowing that this would be a school system that would give my life direction and a solid course to follow throughout my growing years.

What was most difficult, however, was leaving the 'hallowed ground' of schoolyard ball. During the first spring of 1950 I was at a loss as to how to amuse myself.

However, during the month of May word came out in the local papers that merchants in Massapequa were going to establish the first ever Massapequa Little League. This was my new-found hope.

CHAPTER I TRIVIA QUESTION

(Answers found at the end of the book)

How did the now defunct Brooklyn Dodgers get

their team name?

CHAPTER 2
ORGANIZED BASEBALL

I don't really remember how it all began, trying out for a team. Up until this time my baseball experience was based around being "picked up" to play. Although perhaps the guys in Queens were looking at other pick-ups in the neighborhood, I can't remember anyone else hanging around.

When I arrived at Massapequa Elementary School for Little League tryouts, I was surrounded by about seventy-five other prospective players of all sizes and shapes. I also noticed a group of adults, who looked very official walking around carrying clipboards as if they had already started examining the troops. I saw what appeared to be a sign-in table and I waited on line to sign up. When my turn came I answered the basic questions, filled out some forms, and I can't remember if I needed any parental approval or signature. In either case, I would have had to go home since I rode my bike to the try-out session. So I guess no parental permission was needed at the time. Having completed the perfunctory paper work, I was given a piece of cardboard with the number "48" on it, and I pinned it on my shirt. Right behind me in line was Charlie whose last name escapes me and he had "49" on his shirt. For some reason he looked even more nervous than I felt. At that point one of the "clipboard" men told me to go out into the field and get ready to field ten ground balls, no stretching, no warm-ups, no throwing. This was becoming one of the most stressful moments of my life. As I stood out there I noticed one line of children on either side of me. At this point my try-out began. Another man holding a bat and ball started hitting ground balls as the clip board man recorded how many grounders I successfully fielded. I fielded eight out of the ten chances and they weren't too concerned if I threw the ball back accurately to another adult standing to receive my sometimes errant throws.

After fielding eighty percent of my chances, I was told to go to the line on my left. I quickly figured out that the line on my right was for the children who hadn't been as successful. As I stood there, I witnessed Charlie's tryout which unfortunately wasn't as successful as mine and he was sent to the other line. What I remember most about this was the number on my shirt and the "clipboard" man not only recording my score, but announcing it in a loud voice for all to hear not only in Massapequa, but also I think in Seaford the adjoining town. Charlie had fielded only three out of ten. At this point, I am not too clear on what I did for the rest of the tryouts. I vaguely remember swinging a bat, but I am not sure. We were told to go home and wait for a phone call. I received a call. I was told that I had made it and my team would be called the Firemen. Mr. Molloy, the coach, would contact me about practices, games, etc.

This experience is one that I would take with me as I embarked on my teaching and coaching career, always remembering the faces of some of the kids who weren't as successful. This was serious stuff; organized teams, uniforms, scheduled practices, lined fields, umpires, etc. I wondered to myself whether I would ever just play pick-up games and be allowed to use my creativity. Thinking about this and reducing it to writing in this book, I think I began to and still have reservations about organized youth sport programs at this early age. Although at the time ten years of age was old compared to the current youth programs. My son-in-law, Jim, asked me recently if giving a six-year old pitching instruction was a bit much. I told him that I definitely thought it was! I have always been a proponent of letting kids have fun with baseball early on. They will have time enough to compete at a more serious level as they get older, and if they love what they are doing, they will hone their skills at the proper time to give a good account of themselves in high school, college, and perhaps professional ball at some level.

The 1950 Massapequa Little League was composed of four teams: the Bankers, Comets, Indians, and my team the Firemen. The people who picked the teams did a good job of spreading out the wealth of talent throughout each team, although I thought the Comets might have had an edge. My coach was Mr. Molloy and we had a few practices before opening day. During these practices, I guess I showed some accuracy in the pitching department, so the "crafty lefty" was named to start on opening day! I immediately went home and got my Uncle Eddie to play catch with me. He got home earlier than my Dad and time was of the essence. He was also a devoted Yankee fan, which made our relationship somewhat strained. All I can remember is that my Uncle Eddie had a baseball mitt that looked like five ripe bananas tied together, and I had my trusty Pinky Higgins three-fingered model made by, I believe, the Rawlings Company. I got my pitching practice in and felt a little better prepared to start on the weekend. My Dad also caught me, but his glove looked like a chocolate doughnut, round with a pocket in the middle. This was somewhat disconcerting because when he showed you the target, you always thought that to throw a strike, you had to hit the glove squarely or roundly in the middle. Needless to say, being a lefty I had some natural movement on my ball, hence the ball didn't always hit the target and my Dad had to chase balls that were a little off center. I don't think Johnny Bench would have done any better using that glove to catch with. This practice with my Dad and Uncle Eddie, however, would bode well for me during my first season.

It was opening day, summer of 1950, when I arrived at the field that Saturday afternoon. The first thing I noticed was a snow fence encircling the outfield with red, white, and blue bunting draped all around. Nowadays bunting seems to be a lost art in the American League, and as a National League fan, I just had to mention it in this context. The field was also lined and there was a P.A. system set up behind home plate. It was World Series time and I was somewhat overwhelmed, but too excited to have it bother me. This was serious baseball!

All the other players began to arrive along with their parents and friends. This was the first time that I saw lawn chairs used for watching a sporting event. What a neat idea especially since the existing bleachers left a lot to be desired. Each player congregated with his team and we lined up two teams along each foul line. We were all decked out in our new uniforms and our new sneakers. Mine were black high-top Keds, the choice of many kids who were into the sneaker scene. Everyone had the bill of their baseball cap bent in a "V" formation with some players having creased the top of the hat forming a crown. This was the style of the times and, as you know, it changes every few decades or so. Baseball is a fickle game when it comes to dressing. I also remember seeing some of the iron-on letters coming loose from the flannel shirts, making some team names difficult to discern. I believe that I saw a couple of "_omets" and "_ankers" shirts as we lined up. We were asked to "doff" our caps, salute the flag, and listen to a scratchy rendition of our National Anthem played on a 45 rpm RCA phonograph, the one with the big brown spindle in the middle. Finally, it was time to play ball, but with four teams and only one field, the coaches drew lots to see who would play in the first game and who would have to practice patience watching until the second game was ready to begin. As fate would have it, my team, along with the Indians, were picked to play the nightcap. This had a dual effect on my psyche. I was relieved that I didn't have to perform right away, but I became more nervous as I watched the other teams compete. In fact, I might have gone to the food shack one too many times to gulp down a Mission grape soda! We didn't have any port-a-potties in those days and the school was closed for the weekend. You get the idea.

Finally, we played our game. It may seem strange but I cannot tell you what the outcome of the game was. Again, this was perhaps another inkling of my approach to the game at this level. I was just glad to be involved in this fun experience. At the start of the game I was given a brand new ball to pitch with and would receive another one if one was fouled out of play! This was too much to comprehend as for years the balls I played with usually had black friction tape wrapped around them after a day of playing. I do remember having some success pitching in the game, with my hitting a skill that still needed to be worked on. However, the statistics were overshadowed by all the pomp and circumstance of opening day.

After the game, I went with the team to Wetson's hamburger stand, forerunner to McDonald's, and Coach Molloy treated us to a burger and a soda. I believe the burger cost 15 cents. All in all it was a momentous day for me, one that I would not forget and I was already excited about playing our next scheduled game. However, I would be remiss if I didn't tell you what Mr. Schmidt, the plate umpire, wore as a uniform. He was dressed nattily with his summer whites and an outside open "balloon chest protector" to ward off any foul tips. What a sight! He was very classy. He did miss a couple of calls due to the fact that he had to continually readjust the protector so that he could see over it.

The season continued with weeknight practices and weekend games. Our team won some and lost some, but we improved each and every time we went on the field. After about eight games, the newspaper in town started to publish the top ten hitters in the league on a weekly basis. I had the good fortune to break into the "elite" group (a word I despise), hovering around ninth or tenth throughout the season. My recollection is that Gordon Kelly of the Comets was the league leading hitter. Didn't I tell you that team had more skilled players? At that early time in my baseball life I could already spot good talent. Unbeknownst to us we were asked to compete in yet another level of the game, All-Star competition against other teams representing other leagues on Long Island. I made the team and my Mom proudly sewed the All-Star patch on my uniform sleeve. I still have that patch tucked away somewhere. I think it may be next to a copy of my wedding invitation! The things we keep... although I constantly admonish myself for giving away all of my baseball cards. What was I thinking?

Our first All-Star game was against a team from Bayshore, a town in Suffolk County. Massapequa was the last town on the south shore of Long Island in Nassau County. The game was played at their home field and the ride out east seemed to take forever. Upon driving up to the field, I noticed more lawn chairs and bleachers filled with more people than I had ever seen before. This was somewhat overwhelming, but we played them closely, only to succumb by a score of 3-2. They won the game when a player named Bobby K__, a Polish last name that I couldn't spell, hit one out. I must mention that this wasn't the last time we had to deal with a ball player from Suffolk County of Polish descent. I played the outfield in this game and had the unfortunate experience to see that mammoth drive go directly over my head. We were sad about losing as the winner moved on to the regionals and

Little League baseball on Long Island was on its way. Carl Stotz in Williamsport, PA would be responsible for its final destination.

We continued with our league competition and had a champion declared. The Comets were the eventual league champions. During the course of the summer, the Brooklyn Dodgers were again in the thick of a pennant race and they had a pre-game television show entitled, "Happy Felton's Knothole Gang" on Channel 9. This show invited Little League organizations to pick three players to represent their leagues. During the program you would be introduced to some of the Dodger players, one of which would then take you through a series of throws, ground balls, and fly balls along the right field line in front of the Abe Stark sign at Ebbetts Field. I mention this because the sign was in fair territory and if a Dodger or their opponent were to hit the sign with a line drive, they would win a suit. This wasn't an easy task since the sign was at the base of the right field wall and usually the right fielder, Carl Furillo, was stationed directly in front of it. The chances of the 'Reading Rifle' missing a line drive were very remote. The officers of the Massapequa Little League got in touch with the Dodgers and our league was asked to be on the pre-game program. However, there was one hitch - only three players could be chosen and we had four teams! So the officials in their infinite wisdom decided to draw straws to see which players would be picked to attend. My coach drew the short straw and a representative from the Firemen did not go. I always secretly felt that if my team was chosen that I might have been the player to represent us. In fact, I must admit I had already picked myself so when my team was not selected, I was very disappointed. How presumptuous of me! I gained much humility watching three of my friends compete on TV, talking with Brooklyn Dodgers, and receiving a new bat and glove as gifts. It was time to be above it all and feel happy for them, but I suffered through it especially when they arrived home with their new equipment. Oh well, one of life's curve balls, and I would find out that more would be thrown my way in due time.

One final comment about the summer - rainouts! I despised them and would actually cry if we were postponed due to the weather. I was too prepared to have a game not played, especially after a six-mile ride on my bike to the southwest corner of Massapequa, Long Island, New York!!

CHAPTER 2 TRIVIA QUESTION

How did the saying, "The pitcher just got knocked

out of the box" originate?

CHAPTER 3
ONWARD AND
UPWARD

Since this was the first season ever of Little League Baseball in Massapequa, many of the players including myself were already twelve years of age, hence, too old to continue playing the following year. Due to this, a Babe Ruth League affiliation was formed for thirteen through fifteen year-olds, allowing kids to play at yet another level.

I do not have the same recollection as to how the tryout process went, but again, I was selected to participate. This time I was placed on a team called the Senecas. My memory eludes me as to the names of the other three teams. Once again we had a four team league and I believe that they were also Native American names. The Mohicans and the Iroquois come to mind. Each team was composed of twelve players with a combination of some players from each of the Little League teams. During the tryout period, other youngsters that had moved into town now had the opportunity to make the teams. Another interesting event was taking place during the off-season. Nassau County was booming with home construction, and towns that previously did not have high schools were now seriously considering their options of sending students out of district or establishing their own school systems. The towns of Massapequa and Massapequa Park decided to do the latter. We would continue our education in our own town.

As a seventh-grader I knew then that I would be in the first class to graduate six years down the road, June 1956. This decision had many ramifications, not the least being that we were to have interscholastic athletics starting that spring for the Massapequa Public Schools. We would have an organized program which would prepare us for the summer competition. Being only seventh graders, we played other seventh grade schools in the area that spring.

In the summer my coach was Mr. Cox and our team was composed of, as I look back, a group of 'rawboned" athletes who had the talent to play but needed a lot of fine tuning. Hence, we struggled each season, three to be exact, but each year I was fortunate to make the Babe Ruth All Stars. My position changed to the outfield due to the fact that the previous spring I suffered an arm injury that would not allow me to pitch. The injury was "bone chips" in my pitching elbow which caused me a lot of pain when I threw the ball. Trying to be a proficient hurler was impossible. It is hard to believe but maybe I was the first person on Long Island to have "Tommy John Surgery". They opened up my left elbow, removed the chips, then relocated my ulna nerve, and sewed me up. Remember, now that arthroscopic surgery was not yet invented, I have a scar that looks like a zipper on a jacket showing two lines of sutures inside my left elbow.

Playing that spring proved quite a task since I was still nursing my injury. I played right field and when a ball was hit in my direction, I would field it and immediately under hand it to the centerfielder who would toss it into the infield. My arm finally healed and I could throw overhand without pain. I had a good offensive year and again made the All Star Team. Similar to Little League there were not many leagues established at that time so our journey to the finals in Washington, D.C. at Griffith Stadium would not involve too many games. We knew we had to win our

Long Island Championship, and then win the state tournament to go on to the regionals.

Our first contest pitted us against a team from the east end of Long Island, kids mainly from the town of Bridgehampton. We played them at a neutral site in Suffolk County, Mattituck, and we beat them 8-7 to win the Long Island Championship. One interesting side note about "The Eastenders", as they were called; they had a pitcher/shortstop by the name of Carl Yazstremski. He had pitched the game before the final game so he played shortstop this game and contributed with a grand slam homerun that went out of the park as if it were launched from a booster rocket! I was playing the outfield and watched in close proximity as the ball sailed out into space.

We now moved on to play for the New York State Championship in Mount Kisco, New York. We won both games and were crowned champs. I went 3 for 3 in the championship game (I have to put this in as I never went 3 for 3 again... ever!). It was on now to the regionals to be played in Clarksburg, West Virginia. We were to travel by train and arrangements had to be made immediately. The coaches also had to prepare us for this once-in-a-lifetime experience. My coach, Mr. Cox, was the person in charge, and he was as "rawboned" an administrator as we were players. We finally got our "ducks in order" and were ready to leave Massapequa by train on an August weekend.

Everyone was excited, but I had some extra baggage to take along with me. During the school year I failed the New York State Regents Test in Plane Geometry. I was presently enrolled in a summer school session at Freeport High School to make up for my poor showing in the spring! The course was for six weeks, and one could only miss three classes or one would not be able to get the required credit. I had already missed one class due to the tournament travel, so I had only two excused absences left. This regional tourney was to be a three to four day affair, depending on how successful we were. So I think that you see my conundrum. If we continued to win, I would have to board a train on Sunday evening and return to New York by myself while the rest of the team would continue their quest to reach Washington, D.C.! Believe me, I had NO option. My parents had laid out the money for summer school and I was told that I could go to the tournament, but had to return for summer school, no questions asked. So I departed on this excursion with mixed emotions as to how successful I wanted our team to be.

The trip to West Virginia was long and uncomfortable, but we finally arrived in Clarksburg around ten o'clock that Friday evening. We went straight to the hotel and to bed. All I remember about the hotel was that it was very dark in the hallways and ungodly hot in the rooms. We were scheduled to play Saturday morning. We got up early and ate breakfast, then proceeded to the ball park. This park could have been the movie set for "The Natural", and maybe it was! It was a green wooden edifice with a green wooden outfield fence with knotholes in it. We played and won the first game, took a two hour break, played again and lost, putting us in the losers bracket. That evening all the teams congregated in the hotel lobby and just hung out. As I looked around the room, our team seemed to be the smallest group there. We had a curfew of 10 PM; however, our coaches didn't as was evident by the racket that they made in the hotel hallway around one AM - enough said!

The team we faced on Sunday was from Pennsylvania, and they must have been fed very well in the Keystone State because they were huge, man for man. We had our top hurler on the mound by the name of Eddie Rodriguez. The E-Rod, as he would be called nowadays, had a blazing fast ball and was conveniently wild enough to keep these 'Keystone Kids' off balance. It was the top of the seventh inning and we were winning 4-3 only to have them score two runs to go ahead 5-4. As I trotted off the field for our last at bats, I was consumed with much ambivalence about what I wanted to happen, remembering summer school was waiting!   We went down 1-2-3 and we headed home.

I passed Geometry with an 81% average, doubling the grade that I had received during the school year. Does anyone remember those Amsco Review Books? What a summer, but one that I would and still do remember.

CHAPTER 3 TRIVIA QUESTION

How did the fielding position between second base

and third base get its name?

CHAPTER 4
HIGH SCHOOL AND
COLLEGE YEARS

I went to high school at three different schools, starting at one, which was a small junior high, going on to a second which was really an elementary school complex, and finally entering the new high school the second semester of my junior year. In all cases, these were all new schools, built to accommodate us and also to have them ready for the anticipated enrollment increases.

My high school athletic experience was one where I actually excelled in basketball more than baseball. You could say that I went into "spring slumps" during my junior and senior years, but baseball was in my blood and I had decent years due to my coach, Mr. Ricci. He had been a professional baseball player in the White Sox organization and he was a class act. He wore "suntans" -what khakis were called in those days - a college varsity jacket, and white buck shoes as his coaching attire. He was good with kids and we all respected him. Although my high school baseball career was not outstanding, he was one of the people who introduced me to the idea of going to college. No one in my family had gone to college so this was a new idea for me. In fact I was to become a first generation college student in my family. I graduated in June of 1956 as part of the first graduating class at Massapequa High School, and I began to think about going to Cortland State Teachers College in Cortland, New York. I planned to major in Physical Education. After going up to Cortland in January to take a battery of physical fitness tests, I waited anxiously for an acceptance reply; however, none was forthcoming. This was especially disheartening since two other classmates who had gone with me had already received their acceptance letters in early February. I finally received mine on February 26th which was my birthday. It was given to me by my Mom. She informed me that she had taken it out of the mail two weeks before, but kept it to give to me on my birthday. Mom always liked to surprise people.

Since I was the first child in my family to go to college, I had no idea about the experience I was about to encounter. I couldn't even talk with schoolmates about this venture because we were the first graduating class. So I went to Cortland as a true verdant freshman. I was put on the Long Island Railroad, went into Penn Station, and then took the "tube" to Hoboken, New Jersey, where I boarded an Erie and Lackawanna train entitled the "Phoebe Snow". This trip was to prove to be the circuitous route to Cortland, New York. It began in New Jersey, then into Pennsylvania, then north to Binghamton, New York, and finally to Cortland, New York. I had two grips, luggage, as I boarded. It was a hot, humid, August day, and of course this train had no air conditioning. I remember sitting in a wicker-style seat and sticking my head out the window to breathe some fresh air. I kept my head in when we traveled through the coal country of Pennsylvania.

Upon reaching my destination, it was late afternoon, and I started to walk up the hill to the campus to register and go through an orientation. This college sat on a hill overlooking the beautiful farmland of central New York State. So my walk was straight up hill and I had to stop along the way to readjust the grip on my luggage and to check to see if my arms were worthy of handling the weight. I finally arrived at the summit, got all my paper work completed, and received a red and white freshman beanie. I then walked down the hill to where I was going to live off campus. Perhaps I should have stopped there first and unloaded my things. It would have certainly made the trek up the hill a little easier. What was I thinking? Remember I was a young, naive seventeen year old, who now had to wear this silly beanie anytime he went to school or to town!

The college experience from the onset was overwhelming to me and I often considered getting back on that train and returning to Massapequa Park, New York. But that was not an option, so as the weeks progressed I felt a little better and got through my anxiousness. I guess the main difficulty was that I didn't have anything to do in the fall after classes each day, and when I did have the chance to try out for the freshman basketball team, I was cut on the last day of tryouts. What a blow to my confidence! It was at that time that I vowed when I became an athletic coach I would devise a better process of informing players without using a cut list to see if your name was on it. I was devastated. Didn't they know that I once scored 22 points in a game my senior year in high school? Ah, the pains of growing up.

Baseball tryouts started in February inside the main gym and I was psyched. Playing baseball in central New York from March to May leaves something to be desired. We were of course inside more than outside and the drills became boring. You can only field so many ground balls and hit so many balls off batting tees. This is how we were being evaluated so you had to perform. We didn't have a pitching machine or an indoor batting area so that was it; throwing, fielding ground balls, hitting off tees, and hustle. I made the team! We went outdoors in March, shoveled the snow off the field, and played a twelve game schedule. This was the beginning of my college baseball career.

During the summer I had to work so I really never played any ball. When sophomore season came around the next spring, I tried out for the varsity, only to be placed on the junior varsity for a second year. I guess not playing in the summer kept me from improving my skills. In my junior and senior years I made the varsity and played yet another position, first base. Since I was a shade under five foot ten inches, I wasn't a large target for the infielders to throw to, but I was there learning my new position. Things went well and in our senior year we won the New York State College Tournament.

If it wasn't for baseball, I believe that I would have probably left college and returned home sometime during those four years. That would have been a bad decision since while staying the course, I met a young elementary education major. Her name was Ruth Lord. We dated on and off our junior year, I being the one to almost have this relationship end, due to some "college capers" and indiscretions. We rekindled our dating our senior year and have continued for forty-six years!! We were married in August, 1961 and during this span brought four daughters into the world. They have since married and keep presenting us with grandchildren, with a dozen to date.

CHAPTER 4 TRIVIA QUESTION

How did the "bullpen" get its name?

CHAPTER 5
TEACHING AND
COACHING

I got my first teaching job in Massapequa. Yes, you might say, I returned to the scene of the crime. I was hired as a physical education teacher at a junior high school in Massapequa Park. I started coaching three sports; football, basketball, and baseball. What made this special was that I was going to be receiving a stipend for each coaching position. This was unbelievable, but I didn't refuse the monetary reward, albeit, when I look back it was not much renumeration for all of the time put into the job. However, that was my choice, and I had to tolerate the fact that teachers worked under the ethos of "the labor of their love". Coaching as a career can be very rewarding, yet very time consuming. My real employment was being a physical education teacher, so I had to set my priorities. Was I training to be a professional coach, or teaching the fundamentals of the sports to youngsters, or was it both? I also believe that coaching and teaching are interchangeable so I wasn't abandoning either, however, I must admit I did change my priorities every spring. For thirteen years I gave more time in preparing for my baseball seasons than to my daily teaching job. Baseball still commanded a special spot in my life.

My first baseball coaching position was at a high school in Massapequa, Berner Jr./Sr. High School. During the time I was there my teams had many successful seasons, one being a perfect 22-0 season in 1966. During my stay as the junior varsity baseball coach, I had a few experiences that I feel are worth noting since they, I believe, dealt with the essence of teaching youngsters during their formative years.

I was always attracted to students, who were not athletically gifted, in fact in some cases, educationally challenged, so I would try to help them a little more. One of those students was a player named Ed. He was a strapping young man and a pitcher by trade. Ed, as they say in baseball parlance, could "bring it", but where he brought it was a different matter. He was wild and we had to work on his control. He was truly a reclamation project. Ed was Ed, very inattentive with a funny gleam in his eye. He also would mutter things under his breath when you spoke to him. Coaches worked with him, but he also had his moments. When he wasn't pitching he sat on the bench, talking under his breath to a point where he would have all the players laughing and not paying much attention to the game. Of course he only did this when we were up and I was coaching third base. In fact, I thought of having our dugout/ bench moved to the third base side, so I could hear what was going on. But I decided to leave well enough alone and deal with him at the appropriate time. One time I looked over to the bench and witnessed Ed burying his bat vertically into the ground so only the knob of the bat handle could be seen. However, the most memorable moment was when he was pitching and had all his stuff. He went into the seventh inning not scored upon. He had only given up two hits at that point. All of a sudden Ed proceeded to issue one, two, and then three walks in a row to load the bases, thus putting the opponent back into the game. I called time and went out to speak with him, remembering that it was Ed I would be conversing with. I was ready for anything. I asked him what was up and he informed me that he had deliberately walked those three batters and he now was going to strike the next three out! This was vintage Ed. I left the mound, sat down on the bench, and watched him mow the next three down with strikeouts!! This was one of those rewarding moments, yet unsettling, that one encounters when coaching youngsters.

Another interesting scenario was when I coached family members who made the team on their own merits, namely my brother, Tom, and my cousin, Bob. In retrospect, being a young coach, I didn't give any thought as to how the other players were going to view my coaching of my relatives. They played because of their abilities, and I was fortunate not to have anyone speak to the issue of nepotism. Today one would be sure that all the nuances of coaching your own flesh and blood would be addressed before you embarked on your season. Being politically correct in those days was for politicians only. In sum, we had good rapport and I think everyone enjoyed themselves as members of the team that year. As I remember we didn't have many skilled players, so the season was a work in progress, win some, lose some.

In 1968 I became the varsity baseball coach at Massapequa High School, which was the original high school in our town until Berner High opened in 1961. The population explosion continued on the Island.

We now had two high schools that housed over two thousand students in each building. This was my first varsity coaching position, and I felt ready.

Being a coach at the rival high school, Berner, for seven years, did not make my transition easy. In those days the rivalry was intense between the two schools, which I might mention were both located south of the main highway, only about two miles from each other. So it wasn't North vs. South rivalry, but a situation that at times was too close for comfort. I had five good years at Massapequa High School coaching baseball and during that time was fortunate in winning a divisional championship in 1970 which was instrumental in getting a few players into college to play ball. The 1970 team was an eclectic bunch of kids; some were very studious, some were very creative, and some were two sandwiches short of a picnic, if you know what I mean! To illustrate this we had a relief pitcher who would keep three chocolate-chip cookies tucked in his uniform shirt and every time he got an out, he would take one out and eat it! He was successful at what he did, and kept his weight down by doing a lot of sprints. Another pitcher (by now if you are a baseball fan you must know that pitchers are a group unto themselves) went to M.I.T. in Boston, Massachusetts, and invented a bike lock that was supposedly impenetrable, thus putting a stop to all the bike thieves in the immediate Boston area.

The last anecdote concerning this team is that when you are hot you want to continue playing as momentum is in your favor. Half way through the season we had a stretch of inclement weather and had a few games rained out. We were so intent on getting a game played that I persuaded the opposing coach to come to our field for a Saturday double-header. The field was in poor playing condition, but I promised to have it ready. Friday afternoon we got most of the water off the infield, but as sunset approached we knew we had to get some sand to cover the wet areas. We all met early Saturday morning to continue our field preparation. It was decided that we would take a player's car and go down to the beach (we were near the Great South Bay) and get sand. The kids left in one car and the rest of us continued to address the remaining field conditions. Well time went by and the players hadn't returned. We were about to send another car to the beach, when one of the players came walking back. He went on to tell us that they had filled up Andy's car trunk with sand and as they started back, the rear axle gave way! Someone above must have witnessed this scenario because as we were pondering what to do next, the sun came out and the field dried out by game time. Talk about being committed, this bunch was possessed. Unfortunately, I do not remember the outcome of the games, nor do I remember who paid for Andy's axle. This all seemed secondary to the experience of preparing for a game. We continued to remain in first place in our division, and then the unthinkable happened.

After much negotiating between the Massapequa Teacher's Association and the Massapequa School Board, talks stalled mainly over salary issues. The teachers voted to walk out and strike. Yes, they refused to go into work for eleven days. My baseball team was caught right in the middle of this mess. Being a teacher was my first responsibility and my livelihood, and coaching was secondary. I vacillated back and forth and finally decided to go to work. Having never crossed a picket line before, I did not know what to expect. Well the irony of it all was that the picketers were just as neophyte in their role as I was. So I picked two mild-mannered colleagues, walked up to them, said "good morning", and walked into the building. This situation was not to be taken lightly, and to this day I know that hard feelings still exist. Teaching classes inside was one thing, but it was May and I took my classes outdoors. It was very disconcerting running students through their paces and looking at a line of teachers picketing outside the chain link fence that surrounded the athletic field.

As far as the situation and its effect on my coaching, well it did indeed have an impact. I was told I could not use the baseball field until the strike was settled. Great! We were in the middle of a league season and we had no home field to practice or play games on. I called all the players at their homes, and I arranged to meet with them at an undisclosed site to practice. I knew this action would not sit well with the 'higher ups', but so be it. We needed to practice. However, playing the league schedule was another story. We did luck out in that during this eleven day work stoppage three scheduled games were non-league affairs, so we could cancel them without affecting our league standing. We, of course, had to reschedule our remaining league games which we were able to do during the final weeks of the season. The opposing team I remember was very cooperative, and we prevailed winning our league title only to be eliminated in the second round of the playoffs. This reshuffling definitely played havoc with our pitching staff in the final analysis. The rest of the school year was very interesting to be sure. What an ending!

It was during this time that I came in contact with the second Ed in my baseball life. This young man was a baseball buff when it came to keeping statistics. He always had with him a game that was called, I believe, "Stratomatic Baseball". It was based on compiling statistics of all professional players to be used in playing a board game. He was to become our score-keeper and a friend to all his teammates. His love for the game gave him a role in athletics during his high school years as he, too, was an educationally challenged student. Baseball gave him an outlet to be part of the school scene. I continued coaching until the spring of 1973.

CHAPTER 5 TRIVIA QUESTION

At one time players, upon changing sides, would

leave something on the field. What was it?

CHAPTER 6
SUMMER BASEBALL

After graduating from college my need to play baseball still persisted, so I decided to form a team in Massapequa sponsored by the local Kiwanis Club. I knew of certain friends who also had the passion to compete so we got together and held tryouts. I became the player/coach and "chief bottle washer". This turned out to be an interesting summer and gave me the experience in dealing with adults playing the game. Suffice it to say, there were many egos to deal with and I managed this team for one summer. I then decided to be just a player the following summer joining the Seaford Athletic Club which was a member of the Nassau County Alliance, a semi-pro league. Our coach was a fellow by the name of Vic Morrone. He was paralyzed from the waist down and sat on a milk crate and coached. He also used verbal signals when he wanted us to execute. If he wanted you to steal, he would just call out steal and let the rest take care of itself. No surprises from Vic, and as I look back, we were still competitive and won our share of games; enough of all the hand gesturing and uniform touching, who needed it? I played right field and most of our games were double headers played on Sunday mornings. So as a young married man, I had to work this arrangement out with my young married gal. She was agreeable; however, if we went out Saturday night, getting up to play on Sunday mornings was something of a task.

The summers were hot and playing in the heat of the day sometimes took its toll. This summer was the first time ever that I experimented with chewing tobacco at eleven a.m. in the morning! I stuck a piece in my mouth, jogged out to right field, and promptly swallowed the whole damn thing! What followed was not pretty. And as I watched our pitcher, my close college buddy Chris, begin his warm ups, my situation became serious. Instinctively, I raced into the woods along the right field foul line, took care of what had to be taken care of, and quickly returned in time to see Chris deliver his first pitch. I never tried Red Man again.

Playing baseball allowed me to come in contact with quality people. One such person was George, who I had competed against while I was in high school. He was an outstanding student-athlete both in baseball and basketball at Freeport High School. His college days were spent at Villanova in Philadelphia, where he was equally successful. Unfortunately, George passed away far too early in life from a mysterious blood disease. We had become good summer friends and this was one of those times upon hearing such sad news that you take stock of your own being.

A second incident like this took place when I found out that a high school and college friend who I had played with was diagnosed with bone cancer in his hip. Buddy was an excellent ball player with shortstop being his best position. He and I had attended Cortland State Teachers College in Cortland, New York, but he was so talented that the Los Angeles Dodgers drafted him during college, and he had the arrangement where he would attend CSTC in the fall, and then go to spring training with the Dodgers. He was assigned to Reno, Nevada which was a Class C team. In those days there were four or five minor league levels: single A, double A, and triple A were the top levels prior to the 'biggies'. During his stay at Reno, his hip began to bother him, but he did not let others know about it. In doing so, the Dodgers began thinking that he was 'dogging' it since his performance dropped off dramatically. He was in intense pain, and he finally went to the team doctor who sent him to Los Angeles to be examined. Buddy had married a nurse and she was able to give him the loving care that he needed in the next two years at which time he passed on. Life's ups and downs can come at anytime, and we must accept them and deal with them. This, of course, is more easily said than done and incidents like the ones described above made me realize that life sometimes seems to be unfair. We all will have to face trials and tribulations, no questions asked. This was to be a reminder later on in my personal life. I feel fortunate that I had met these two individuals and used their experiences to help me through my difficult times.

I want at this point as a memorial to Buddy to again ask you, the reader, the following question: "How did the shortstop position get its name?" The answer is at the back of the book. Don't peek unless you have read enough of this book and want to put it down!

As mentioned before, I had yet another Ed enter my life. He was my brother-in-law and was always fun to be around. Albeit, some of our antics weren't always received well by our significant others. One Sunday I asked Ed if he wanted to join me to watch one of my Seaford AC games. He said fine and we arrived early, in fact a lot earlier than most of the players. This was a thing with me, to show up early to get prepared to play, not just show up five minutes prior to the start of the game. This ritual still continues today, as I ask my players to do the same. Ed also questioned why we had arrived so soon, but he endured. As I was going through my routine of getting the cobwebs out of my aging body, I was approached by a man who handed me a business card. He was a scout from the San Francisco Giants. He told me that he had seen me play in a few games that summer and liked what he saw. It's funny because I always thought I was at least a year behind in my physical development, and at this time of my life I had finally reached my potential. The reason for this catch up in maturation probably had to do with my doing the third and fourth grades in one year at P.S. 108. Remember those educational experts, they struck again! I never knew the exact reason for this consolidation of classes, but I was chosen! So here I was, out of school, married, teaching, and soon to be a father for the first time. This was too much to handle on a Sunday morning being scouted for the major leagues. Dream on Pete Michel, dream on. The kicker was that in the first inning of play, I got tossed for arguing vehemently with the umpire. So this guy came all the way from San Francisco to see his next phenomenon get thrown out. He really lived close by and was a 'bird dog' scout, who is not on a team payroll, but will occasionally find a diamond in the rough. I was not to be his fortune this time.

On the way home Ed was in a state of shock. He couldn't understand the actions of his crazy brother-in-law. It was a missed opportunity, but so it goes. We lost Ed at the age of forty-eight, succumbing to a heart attack. Again I paused to take stock of my life. When your contemporaries are the ones that are dying, you take more time to smell the flowers, or as the late singer-song writer Warren Zevon aptly stated prior to his death, "Enjoy each sandwich".

Memorial Day, 1962, proved to be a seminal moment in the relationship of Ruth and Pete Michel. It was the first time that the Los Angeles Dodgers ("O'Malley, you bum!") were returning to New York to play our soon to be beloved and later 'amazin' Mets. The double header, a tradition that has now ended, was to be played at the Polo Grounds. I got tickets and dragged 'Rudy' with me. She was now three months pregnant with Beth and to keep her comfortable we brought a foam kitchen chair pad for her to sit on. If you have ever been to the Polo Grounds you knew that it wasn't fan friendly, especially for the lady patrons. The bathroom facilities being like hen's teeth, few and far apart. Upon getting there you had to 'queue' up for some time. This was not a pleasurable thought for a pregnant woman, especially for a two game affair.

We sat in the left field seats which actually overhung the field so that you couldn't see the left fielder. In fact this was the same area where in the fall of 1951 Bobby Thomson hit the 'shot heard around the world' against the then Brooklyn Dodgers. On that day eleven years prior, I watched on television with my Mom in disbelief and promptly went outside and ran my Schwinn bike into a tree!

The first game began and was won handily by the Dodgers, I believe 13-6. This was a good game for these 'amazin' Mets of the Marv Throneberry era to score six runs, and if memory serves me right, off Sandy Koufax or Don Drysdale. I think it was Sandy as we got to him early, but once he found his twelve to six curve ball, the rest of the game was firmly under his control. During that game the Mets also made history by hitting into a triple play. At the onset of the second game, tragedy struck. Ruth, after finally enduring the walk to and from the ladies' room smelled something burning. Lo and behold her foam cushion was ablaze! A spectator behind her had been depositing his cigar ashes on the cushion and finally spontaneous combustion took place. The spectator promptly doused the burning cushion with a beer. The Dodgers won the second game and we all left wedging ourselves through one of the too few exits in the park. In fact, we were like sardines in a can, which I thought led to a pickpocket's paradise! What a day and what a gal, two gals really! Beth was there too!

CHAPTER 6 TRIVIA QUESTION

By what other name was the New York Giants' Polo

Grounds known as?

CHAPTER 7
JOURNEY TO NEW ENGLAND

After teaching and coaching for thirteen years, in the fall of 1973 I made my first career change. Having received my Master's Degree at Hofstra University in Educational Administration, I embarked on a career in athletic administration. After a few interviews, some of which I got called back for a second time, I received a phone call from the superintendent of schools in the Barrington, Rhode Island school district. They offered me the position of Coordinator of Physical Development. At first the title baffled me somewhat, but at the age of thirty-four, full speed ahead. The job description was to supervise all physical education teachers, coaches in the school district, and to watch over summer recreation activities that would be offered in the schools.

This was to be a sea change for the Michels, who now were six. After Beth we had Amy, Meg, and Jo born to us. If I accepted, and I did, the first change to occur was that I had to leave them in September, '73, while Ruth tried to sell our home on Long Island along with holding down the fort! Everything finally worked out and we were all back together by Thanksgiving in Little Rhody. Leaving my colleagues in Massapequa, many of whom I worked with and coached with for thirteen years, was difficult, but I was given a great send off and I was excited. During the time I was preparing to move on, my old baseball coach, Mr.Ricci, who was now assistant principal said to me, "Pete just remember the higher up you go in education, the less decisions you will make, or be allowed to make on your own." This statement, although I didn't believe it at the time, was to prove to be true later on in any school district where I was to become an administrator. In retrospect, I believe I saw a little sadness in Mr. Ricci's eyes. Oh how right he was!

I thought being the head guy in athletics would allow me, with staff input, to deliver the best physical development program that the district wanted. So having waited a short time to start implementing my ideas (perhaps I should have waited longer), I started recommending different ideas with input from the staff under my direction. The word that was first introduced to me during my deliberations was 'consensus'. In each and every meeting concerning program change a consensus had to be reached by all the parties involved. My staff and I agreed on most ideas, but the upper administration, for the most part, put a damper on them. I defined the word consensus as: "at which no formal decisions are arrived but one implements to which one fails to agree". I never had a clear mandate given to me. Being a 'stubborn Dutchman' and also a flying one as a Hofstra grad, I constantly met opposition with ideas that I felt were good for kids.

Probably the first major issue was dealing with a new federal mandate called Title IX. This mandate basically stated that there should be equal opportunity for males and females to experience athletic endeavors. I read the edict with much interest, and instead of being reactive as many males were inclined to be at that time, I decided to be proactive and bring us in compliance with what had to be done. At this juncture in 1973, it was basically dealing with field usage at the high school. I recommended that the women's field hockey team be allowed to play their home games on the football field. Well, all hell broke loose. I was a football coach for thirteen years and what I was suggesting was pure heresy. The powers that be (I wasn't involved) decided to interpret the federal mandate in a different manner. The status quo prevailed and I was miffed because I believed in sharing the wealth and in this case the turf.

What a visionary! This experience was one of many I encountered in my next sixteen years of administrating in public school systems. I will not bore you with any more, but I sincerely believe to this day had cooler heads prevailed early on, the Title IX battle between the sexes could have been dealt with in a more efficacious manner. There have been many philosophies in interpreting it, some of which have been misconstrued. To this day, there is still not a clear-cut mandate. In fact, recently, President George W. Bush appointed a committee to revisit the federal ruling and review all its implications and ramifications.

As far as doing any coaching during my years as an administrator, the opportunities were few, but I did find time usually during the summer. I coached American Legion Baseball for two years. This coaching experience was to be a challenge as we had a team composed of just a dozen players which didn't give us much depth, but we stayed competitive. Legion ball in Rhode Island is very competitive and we had all to do to hold our own. In some cases our team looked like a Babe Ruth team in stature and strength compared to the teams we were up against. Most recently, I have had the opportunity of coaching other American Legion teams, Senior Babe Ruth teams, and AAU teams in communities where I have lived.

In my final years as a guidance counselor, I coached a seventh and eighth grade team at the local middle school for three years. I always felt that by doing this coaching, I was giving back to the community as well as allowing kids to see me in a different light which had some redeeming carryover features during the school year.

CHAPTER 7 TRIVIA QUESTION

At one time home plate was what geometric shape?

CHAPTER 8
THE JOY IS IN THE STRUGGLE

During my initial administrative job in Rhode Island, I started to become aware of the fact that at times I would get down in the dumps for no apparent reason. I chalked it off to my new environment, this being a tough transition for the entire family, but things just didn't seem right, and the moods became more frequent and intense.

At that time, although Ruth and I didn't know it, I was probably starting to deal with depression. I continued to have episodes of extreme melancholy that would keep me from getting out of bed in the morning and going to work. This was in 1973 and to actually admit this was a disease wasn't yet in vogue. In fact, presently some of us still deal with this with some stigmas attached, but we are making inroads and headway in dealing with clinical depression. I initially went for a complete physical. I was given a clean bill of health, but I have to admit that during my time with the physician I did not mention anything about my mood swings. Things would go along swimmingly, and then I would start to get what I would characterize as 'analysis paralysis' which meant that I became obsessed with the way I was feeling and what could be causing it. Unless you have ever experienced this personally, all I can say to describe it is that you almost become comatose as you try to conduct your daily life. I was able to tolerate it on vacations or during the summer, but at the work place it became a problem.

Adding to this malaise was the fact that my job responsibilities as Coordinator of Physical Development were being evaluated by the school board to see if they wanted to continue this administrative set up. All four coordinator positions were being reviewed and as middle management we were caught between the teachers and the administrative association, not a good place.

Everything came to a head when on Christmas Eve morning, 1974. I picked up the Providence Journal to see the following story on the front page. The headline read, "Coordinators at Local High School Not Certified by the State Education Department to Administer Their Duties". It was true that of the three new coordinators, the other was already a teacher within the school system, I was the only one with public school teaching and administrating credentials. This was not to say that the others were not qualified to carry out their responsibilities. They just weren't certified. Each had doctorates in their specific area of expertise. We became the constant lead story in the local paper as everyone followed our travails to see the outcome. As the spring semester progressed the two coordinators with doctoral degrees left to go elsewhere in the private sector. It was now evident that those vacated positions were not going to be filled anytime soon, if ever. So I continued administering to the athletic coaches and physical education staff with less and less credibility.

I started to meet more resistance from within when I tried to promote new programs. In fact, I was receiving very little staff input and no backing from the administrators. There was a leak in the dike, so to speak, and my position continued to become less credible. I had made some good friendships in school with coaches that I had hired and other professionals who assisted me in managing the nuts and bolts of athletic events. Finally, I was informed by the superintendent of schools that if this administrative plan was to be eliminated, then I would be found a teaching position somewhere within the system. I was somewhat relieved, but I also knew the reason why this structure was being dismantled. I wasn't getting any assistance from the administration and this whole plan was originally school board-driven with the expressed intent of assisting the administration to make improvements to the system. The current board thought that this was not happening. School boards change as did this one, and new agendas are established. The outgoing board had a vision which we were supposed to implement, but it did not succeed.

I resigned my position in 1976 under much fanfare, which I did not invite, and everything died down very quickly. There was a ground swell of support given to me by people who either just liked me or believed I was doing a good job and were on the same page with me philosophically and educationally. I guess the tendering of my resignation might have been somewhat of a 'knee jerk' decision, but I wanted to make a statement and it probably would have been more prudent to do it with another position in place.

I became unemployed in the educational field for the first time, but interestingly enough I was able to receive unemployment benefits. I was told by the officers at the Employment Security Agency, that people didn't usually receive benefits if they resigned a position, only if they were fired or if the job was eliminated. The exception being if the reason for my leaving had to do with my ability to do my job. They reviewed my circumstances and made a favorable decision. This convinced me to some degree that being steadfast in explaining my reasons for resigning was being heard.

This was not a sugar coated scene. I was looking for a job, having a mid-life crisis of sorts, and the depressive episodes were continuing. I tried different options, counselors, psychologists, and finally I went and spoke to a psychiatrist. This was an unnerving experience to go to a 'shrink' with no malice toward that profession, but you know the reality of what most people think whether informed or uninformed. Being able to discuss your innermost emotions and feelings, revealing those hidden demons with a stranger, is not an easy task. Solutions don't happen overnight to begin the healing process. You do not get a cast put on your broken emotions!! Unfortunately the prescribing of drugs to alleviate this condition was not readily available yet. I did however start to have some relief about fourteen years later when I was given a prescription for Prozac. I believe that I must have been one of the first to use this as the drug of choice. In fact, maybe, I could have been the poster boy for it.

Although on paper fourteen years may not seem like an eternity, believe me, it was. My immediate family and I dealt with much upheaval. This demon, depression, made me very compulsive and I reacted to situations without much forethought. I would have 'flight' instead of 'fight' responses as my remedy. I started to leave jobs thinking those situations were the cause of my discontent, and of course that was not the reason at all. Ruth and the kids hung in there with me, but at one point one of my daughters asked me, "Dad, when are you going to keep a job and not pull us up again?" The constant moving was apparently taking its toll on them.

The next move was back to Long Island. I took a job again as an athletic administrator. I assumed this position for three years, but due to the politics of public school administration, I became disenchanted. After family discussions, we decided to move back to New England. In retrospect, the first issue should have been me dealing with my condition; however, this would come later.

So, in the summer of 1979, we took a vacation in Maine and traveled to Augusta to find what educational jobs were available. I had a few interviews, but one job that looked particularly interesting I couldn't interview for since the principal was on vacation. We returned to New York with a call later that week to come back to Maine for an interview.

This is when yet another Ed entered my life. Ed Forbush was the principal and as soon as we met, we hit it off. I accepted the job as assistant principal/athletic director of a small high school in Maine and started the job in September, leaving Ruth to care for the home front.

Ed Forbush, whether he knows it or not, is the reason the Michel family finally settled down in New England permanently. Ed is a true friend, one who knows ones faults, but doesn't give a damn. He is a true "Renaissance" man. We continue to enjoy each other's friendship.

One redeeming feature about this move was that Ruth became gainfully employed as an elementary school teacher. She continues to teach fourth grade, still enjoying teaching and challenging the youth of today.

To bring all of this to some closure, the only thing that continued to give me the balance that I still needed in my life was when I would coach baseball in the summer. I would be myself again. This was a comforting feeling, and I was home again, outside, coaching kids. So to this day, I still am dealing with depression, with a much better plan. I am grateful at my age to have the opportunity to still be engaged in a vocation for which I am passionate. I continue to have the energy required to work with college kids, and my health is such that I can handle the rigors of the job and all that goes with it. I guess the "joy is in the struggle", a phrase that I first heard in Rhode Island when I attended a self-help seminar and the guest speaker made this the title of his keynote address.

I would be remiss if I didn't tell you that you cannot do this alone. You need support. The first step toward this is to put your pride in your back pocket and ask for help. People are there for you and all you have to do is reach out. While I was finishing my educational career as a school counselor having returned to college to get a Masters degree in counseling in 1987, I almost had a 'flight' relapse again. I had a tough school year and I was about to quit and run from reality. However, the principal at the school, who was a very special person, allowed me to return one day after I had sent in my resignation. This person is still a friend for whom I will always have a special fondness. He too had his ups and downs in education, but he always put kids first. Isn't that why you should enter the education field?

CHAPTER 8 TRIVIA QUESTION

What nautical saying was sometimes used when
announcing the batting lineups at the start of each
inning?

CHAPTER 9
COLLEGE COACHING

My first experience coaching college age players started when a friend, who was an athletic director, hired me to coach at a small college in Maine. This was to be a brief experience since within a year the college closed its doors due to a lack of enrollment and mismanagement of funds. However, I got a taste in working with college kids. They were, to be sure, foot loose and fancy free, and I had to immediately corral their energies to the baseball field. We started the fall program, the first ever, and practiced and played our games at a town field. This field was steeped in baseball tradition, having been (as the locals professed) the field where Babe Ruth, while barnstorming in the summer, wore a Red Sox uniform. The story continues as most baseball stories do, that he also hit a home run over the right field fence. To this day there is a little store called "Babe's Place" that is still in business directly behind that right field fence.

While embarking to our first practice, we got into our vans to take us downtown. This van had swing out windows so the kids opened them up as it was a hot, humid, September morning. I was not aware that they had done this, and as I tried to negotiate between two buildings, all I heard was the shattering sound. I looked into the rearview mirror only to see the players covered with shards of glass. They thought it was hilarious. "Way to go, coach" I believe was their response. On Monday morning upon coming to work, I was informed that the President of the college wanted to see me. While talking to him, he informed me that I would have to pay for the damage to the van. They did not have any insurance to cover these types of situations. It was then and there that I knew this institution was suffering from a malady that I would like to characterize as "fundsalow". Say it slowly and you'll get what I mean!

During this time of my life I decided to pursue a masters program in counseling to hopefully secure a school counselor's position at one of the local school districts in the area. Living in a college town afforded me the opportunity of attending a college in my own backyard. This was convenient and less costly. I enrolled part-time at the University of New Hampshire. During this time I worked as a school supervisor at a local high school and then became an assistant principal at an area Catholic school.

The first position allowed me to do a lot of my college class work at the job site as my main function was to conduct what was to be a silent study hall of sorts. The students delegated to my room were those that were having difficulty adjusting to the regular school scene. The concept being instead of suspending them out of school for infractions that didn't warrant suspensions, they would bring their school assignments to my area and spend the entire school day with me. Sometimes it was more than one day. Repeated offenders were dealt with in a different way since their behavior still was not changing in relation to how they approached their studies during the school day. They even had their lunch delivered to them or in some case 'brown-bagged' it. They were allowed bathroom privileges during the times when classes were in session and the hallways were less crowded. This scene might appear like a prison atmosphere with kids being incarcerated, but surprisingly I was able to get some things accomplished with some of these students. They had their classroom assignments to do and then I would have group discussions on many different subjects. Believe me; the range of issues was very interesting. This experience allowed me to work on some of my counseling skills giving me an internship experience.

During this time I was hired as the assistant baseball coach at the University of New Hampshire. I had met the head coach during the past summer while I was coaching a senior Babe Ruth team in town. I went to him to get some input as to what kind of baseball programs existed at the high schools in the area. We immediately hit it off and in the spring of 1982 I was coaching third base in a Wildcat uniform. We were a Division I team playing in what was once called the Yankee Conference, composed of all the state universities in the six New England states. I stayed with Ted Conner for ten years learning new things about coaching. I was always learning and to this day, I still am. Coaching at UNH was very rewarding and at times eye opening. Some of the most memorable experiences never occurred on the field of play as I will elaborate on later. Our season in the spring consisted of playing approximately thirty games, most of them being league contests.

We started our practice sessions inside during the first week of February in an indoor area called the Paul Sweet Oval. In March we went south during the college spring break. As a coach in the Northeast, one must be creative because the first time you usually get outdoors is in late March.

Preparing for a southern trip is a large undertaking. Let's set the scene. We are going to drive approximately twenty college aged men in vans to Florida. Later on we did have a few trips where finances allowed us to fly. Where we would be playing was no where near any beaches or for that matter, bikinis! Our home for one week was in Sanford, Florida, in the middle of nowhere. It has since become a bigger metropolis with a nice airport used as an alternative for travelers to Disney. It is also where the Amtrak Autotrain ends its route. Leaving New England in March and arriving in Florida takes about thirty hours of straight driving to get there. Upon arriving you quickly take off your winter gear and begin to feel the humidity in the sultry South. Our bodies usually adjusted within a day or two, but who cared? The reality was we were outside and playing ball. This complex was run by a man, Wes Rinker, whose famous slogan was "Wes Rinker's Baseball School, where you learn to throw a round ball square." This quote always needed some clarification but once he explained it, it was baseball sound. We played two games a day and also had field areas to practice on. This is what we wanted because we needed as much practice outside as we could get. We never knew what was awaiting us upon our return to New England. In fact, I kept my phone calls home to a minimum as I had a difficult time telling Ruth it was 80 degrees and sunny while she informed me that they had just gotten six inches of snow.

As far as our experience playing, we were always competitive and we got a lot accomplished. The funny thing about this was when we played our first game, we usually hit the ball all over the lot, scoring in double digits and winning most times. I truly believe the reason for this was that we saw the ball as if it were the size of a volleyball because it just looked so much larger than what we had seen in the darkness of Paul Sweet Oval. In due time 'van lag' would set in and we would start to struggle a bit, especially against teams that were from the south who had already played a full complement of games. However, we usually rebounded and took home a couple of trophies.

The main field that we played our games on was originally the New York Giants spring training camp during the 40's and 50s. It had a covered grandstand from first base around to third base. It was painted in bright colors and had a grass infield with only the cut-outs around the bases exposing dirt. The whole field in fact was grass except for the base areas, home plate, and the pitcher's mound. The reason for this was that it drained better after a storm than any other clay or sand mixture. It should be noted that we did have to deal with occasional rainouts, but Wes did his best to reschedule even if it was at eleven PM! In one area along the right field grandstand, seats were painted a different color with a pipe railing cordoning off from the rest of the stands. This section in the old days was for African Americans only and for some reason they continued to keep it that way perhaps for historical purposes.

Wes Rinker was sort of a carnival guy and he would have different events scheduled for the coaches each evening. One of these was an air balloon ride in which he had all the coaches partake. He had an air balloon tethered behind the right field fence. He would ask us to ascend in this colorful contraption. We also were fed between games, and I can still taste the bologna sandwiches that we had at noon time during the heat of the day. There wasn't a tree in sight so the luncheon meat had to be eaten quickly, followed by soda pop that wasn't exactly what your stomach was looking for. As far as eating as a team, Wes gave us tickets to go to the local smorgasbord, called "Duffs". It was there that the players gorged themselves, much to the chagrin of the coaches. I must admit I had my share of chocolate mousse for dessert. In our off time we allowed the players to stay at poolside or in their rooms which by the end of our stay, began to look like the rooms in their frat houses on campus. If the weather was inclement, the team would go to the nearest mall to take in a movie, or as the coaches later found out, the guys would visit the shopping center perfume counters to have conversations with the attractive help. We also had some household chores to do each day. Our pitchers were assigned to laundry detail and went to the local laundromat. The fields that we played on had Georgia clay around the base areas and it proved to be a difficult task to get those uniform stains out. In fact sometimes the 'unis' came back a light pink. Our pitchers hadn't yet mastered the amounts of detergent and stain remover needed to do the job.

As far as our day went, we were always scheduled for a few night games, or we went to see other teams play after supper. We would always have a team meeting at ten o'clock which usually lasted about twenty minutes, then curfew at eleven, and lights out at midnight. As coaches we thought this to be a reasonable time schedule knowing that we had to be 'bright eyed and bushy tailed' each morning for an early team breakfast.

As I stated earlier, being responsible for young adults on a trip like this can be a daunting task. We were to find this out on one of our trips. Our motels were usually situated around strip malls, which on inclement days served as a functional part of the trip. The one part of being 'en loco parentis' sort of speaking was during the evening hours and bed check. We told the players what our expectations were and trusted them to adhere to our wishes. We would take one swing around the motel at eleven thirty asking the room captains if everyone was accounted for. We would then retire for the night. Well on one occasion some of our players decided not to respect the rules and went out on the town. One of our assistant coaches, who happened to be at a 24 hour convenience store picking up ice for the pitchers' arms, met up with seven of our players who were not where they were supposed to be. This coach was between a rock and a hard place, but upon returning to our room told us what had transpired. It was decided that they would report to us the next morning for explanations. We heard what they had to say and after some deliberation, the head coach decided they would not participate in any more games for the remainder of the week. They were also informed that a final decision as to their status for the rest of the spring season would be made upon returning to campus.

Yes, I once was a kid, but as an educator I was clearly aware of the responsibilities given to me by the University and the parents of these players, trusting us to care for the safety of their children. It is unfortunate that youthful indiscretion challenges this responsibility. I must note this and it is important that a few days before this incident, three players from another college were struck by a car late at night as they crossed the highway by this motel. Fortunately they were not seriously hurt. So this was on our minds to the point that we had mentioned it at a prior team meeting.

Upon returning home, the final decision was to continue the suspension for the rest of the spring semester. This led to much finger pointing, copping-out and agitated discussion by those who were directly affected. Interestingly, no one was concerned that by holding to this decision our team was without the services of some skilled players. This caused us to ask other people to step up and perform, which they did. The finality being, we subscribed to the saying, "Eliminate all players with poor attitude regardless of ability."

Aside from what happened on the field, I became very close to some of the players and as an assistant coach, I took on the responsibility of being a sounding board. This comes with the territory and since I also was a school counselor, I enjoyed this part very much. I counseled them about other issues not just relating to baseball and felt fortunate that they confided in me. My ability to offer some support and direction was very rewarding. I also at times was able to be the mediator between the head coach and the players on certain occasions when there needed to be some compromise. As a product of the fifty's and a coach during the sixty's and seventy's, I too had to revisit my beliefs and try to listen to what the players were saying. Sometimes the generational gap between athlete and coach does not allow for much "wiggle room". Having said this, I don't mean to imply that there aren't certain values one must learn. These can be addressed through athletic endeavors. Respect, teamwork, caring, trust, and punctuality, to name a few, are basic tenets that, as a coach, I want to instill in my players. There are many other extra curricular offerings that can accomplish the same, so I am not suggesting that athletics is the 'be all and end all'.

We are all too aware of unscrupulous happenings that have their genesis in the athletic arena. Coaching is a demanding, detailed, sometimes daunting profession if one wants to give more to those under their direction than just W's!

CHAPTER 9 TRIVIA QUESTION

Who played for the Brooklyn Dodgers, New York
Giants, and the New York Yankees?

CHAPTER 10
WILDCAT MUSINGS

At this point I would be remiss if I didn't relate a few stories that were very amusing. In fact, I'll put them in the priceless category.

The first one has to do with two players who missed the bus as we were departing from a hotel in New Haven, Connecticut where we had played Yale the previous day. We were now going on to play The University of Rhode Island. We always had room captains who were responsible for themselves and two other roommates. This responsibility was delegated to players who worked well with their teammates and were willing to accept this responsibility which required them to make sure their room was left in good condition, at least like it was when they entered it, and make sure their roomies got on the bus. As the head coach boarded the bus, he said, "Captains check", which meant make sure everyone was accounted for. Upon hearing no negative responses, off we went. There are many traditions that have a life of their own and on the bus. The head coach always sat on the first seat to the right of the bus aisle. This seat location gives one the most leg room so rank has privilege. I, on the other hand, sat directly behind the bus driver and, I must admit that during the course of many trips, I always watched how the driver was operating the bus just in case something happened and I needed to take control of the wheel. During my travels I had seen many, how should I say it, "Ralph Kramden" types. Hence, I was always concerned about the big H. A. (heart attack).

You see, one can get bored on these trips and start to think of the ridiculous to the sublime. As I was sitting in my favorite seat with very little leg room, one of our players knelt down next to me and whispered in my ear to come to the back of the bus. I got up and went back as if to use the bathroom. It was there that I was told that two of our players didn't make the bus. The person telling me was the room captain so we had a huge problem to deal with. I didn't even ask him how this could have happened as we had to think quickly on our feet. I returned to the front of the bus, but sat down next to the Sports Information Director, whose seating arrangement was three rows back with one seat for him and the other seat for all the computer and statistical paraphernalia. S.I.D.s, as they are called, are a different breed with very creative ideas. Unfortunately, he was not able to offer anything to this ever-increasing problem. I returned to my seat and decided to let things just play out. Here I was trying to cover for a kid who didn't do his job and two kids who were somewhere on the Connecticut Turnpike between New Haven CT and Kingston, Rl.

As we arrived in the parking lot at URI, I noticed a car pull up next to us on my side. I looked out of the window and saw our two players getting out of a car driven by an older woman. I realized it was them and since the head coach was the last to depart from the bus, I got out along with the Sports Information Director. We ran around the front of the bus to tell them that the head coach did not know of their dilemma and immediately had them go around the back of the bus to the other side. When the bus driver opened the luggage compartments under the bus, they got in line and pretended to do the same. What timing!! Later on we had to ask them who drove them from New Haven. We came to find out that a lady hotel worker agreed to take them for ten dollars. College kids, when necessity calls, can be very resourceful.

One final bus experience happened as we were driving to Vermont to play UVM. It was early Friday evening as we were traveling along Route 89. A red light appeared on the bus dashboard and the bus driver stated that the 'skidder valve' was malfunctioning. He then proceeded to tell us that we would have to pull off the highway and radio for assistance, the reason being that we didn't have any breaking power going downhill. I think I mentioned we were in Vermont which is known for its Green Mountains and scenic highways so we had many miles of downhill portions of highway yet to travel.

This was prior to cell phones so we had to get off at a rest area and call. We were told that no one could get to us until the morning. We were then told if we stayed at forty miles per hour the bus could be driven without our lives being endangered. So, we crawled into Burlington at midnight, ending a six hour drive. The next day a repair man from the bus company showed up at the motel and installed a new 'skidder valve'. As I remember we had a successful series against the Catamounts.

Another story involved the Sports Information Director and me. This incident again took place in the state of Rhode Island. We had a successful spring and now were competing in the NCAA Regionals being held at McCoy Stadium in Pawtucket, Rhode Island. Mike, the S.I.D., had made reservations for the team to stay at the Marriott Hotel in Providence and we arrived there on Friday evening and went directly to our rooms. Mike and I were roomies and after watching enough Sports Center on ESPN, it was time to hit the hay. As we both were getting ready to retire, I looked above Mike's bed and saw what appeared to be a wet spot on the ceiling. After closer examination, I noticed that some droplets of water had formed and within minutes, the ceiling got very gray in color and water started to gush out on to the bed! After some laughing, then astonishment, we called down to the front desk to inform them of our dilemma. In the meantime, the water was now cascading down and Mike's bed resembled a non-traditional water bed. Just then the hotel manager knocked on our door to tell us that they had gotten to the source. It seemed that the occupant above us started to draw his bath and evidently fell fast asleep, failing to take a bath or, for that matter, turn the water off. To add to the confusion, the hotel people couldn't awake him so they had to use a pass key to enter the room. They implied that he had been out on the town, and was sleeping his night off in a deep slumber.

Okay, but what about us? I like Mike, and have a lot of respect for him and like to be around him, but I wasn't about to climb under the "blankies" with him. The hotel worker told us the hotel was full except for a few suites that were available. So you guessed it. We went up to the next floor and opened the door to our new digs. We had more room there than we needed. We even had an automatic shoe shiner which I thought was kind of neat. We slept well. Did I mention that there were two TV's? When we woke up we again looked at all the amenities that we didn't take advantage of.

At the team breakfast we had a hard time containing ourselves as we related our story to the head coach and players. Mike, always looking for a good story, got in touch with the Boston Globe to see if this incident was newsworthy. Well about two weeks later we made the <u>Boston Globe</u> Sports Brief section on Sunday. The title of it being, "How Suite It Is". The brief story detailed how we were rained out of our room, but not our game. Good stuff, and

Mike still has the room key as a memento from our adventure!

All in all it was an interesting weekend. We did play baseball; lost to the University of Maine on Saturday after leading by the score of 3-0 in the first inning when our right fielder hit a homerun off Billy Swift. That was all we could muster as Billy Swift's slider became unhittable and we lost 10-3. In the loser's bracket, we had the University of Connecticut by the score of 8-5 in the last inning only to be beaten by a walk off grand slam homerun!! Baseball... it was invented to be a game that breaks one's heart.

One last postscript about coaching at UNH: we once played a triple header. Yes, we played three. Ernie Banks would have loved it!

CHAPTER 10 TRIVIA QUESTION

What was the original name of the Brooklyn

Dodgers when they were first organized?

CHAPTER 11
DEALING WITH A
DEMON

I continued coaching at UNH for a couple of more years and then became the head coach at Keene State in Keene, New Hampshire. This college had terminated their program ten years earlier so it was my task to bring the program back. Having gained valuable experience at UNH, I was up to the task. In the fall of 1986 I met with the prospective players. They had a club team the past spring so I had a core group of players to work with. We held tryouts and played a fall schedule. We were successful and anxiously looked forward to the spring when we would be playing at the NCAA Division II level. Having not been able to do much recruiting, I sent out letters to all the state public and private high school coaches explaining our new baseball program. I went about seeing prospective players and talked with them and their parents about baseball at Keene.

My office was in the swimming pool area of the field house, not the best place to conduct business. It was always humid and even with portable fans it was tough to be there for any length of time. So at times I felt disenfranchised from the rest of the coaching staff who had their offices in the front of the field house. I handled it as best as possible and went along preparing for the spring season. Recruiting picked up and I had a few students interested in coming. We even had some scholarship money to give them.

At the same time I was able to finish my master's internship in counseling by working for the College Counseling Services. This was an interesting experience mainly dealing with students who were having difficulty transitioning into college life and all that goes into it. I had a daily schedule set up in the counseling center and met with students for thirty minute appointments. I even had some of my ball players come for some advice. I was also asked to teach some physical education classes. These classes were for students who had to fulfill a physical education requirement to graduate. I taught beginning tennis and badminton. This was very enjoyable and I received a stipend for this along with my coaching check. It wasn't much, but I knew, with Ruth who was still teaching, this was doable and only a temporary situation. I was led to believe that there was an opportunity to become fully employed in the near future. They had talked about me joining the Physical Education faculty as I already had one masters in education and was completing another. My bachelor's degree in Physical Education complemented my background.

The traveling time between Durham and Keene was about one hour and forty-five minutes' west driving hill and dale to get there. New Hampshire's highway system is laid out north to south probably so tourists can get to the ski areas quickly in winter and the leaf peepers can get there in the fall. So as the saying goes in this part of the country, "You can't get there from here". I occasionally stayed over at my sister-in-law's house which was half way. It was there that I sat and watched the 1986 World Series Game 6 between the Red Sox and the NY Mets. My sister-in-law started to watch this with me only to retire before the ending and then to be rudely awakened by her crazy brother-in-law screaming at the top of his lungs as a ground ball went through Bill Buckner's legs down the right field foul line. I had been in New

England since 1979, but I was still a committed Met fan, hence, my exaltation. The first semester ended as did my teaching responsibilities and I planned a February meeting for all prospective candidates interested in trying out for the spring season.

It was at that time that I was told I wasn't being considered for full time status on the faculty because of a philosophical difference between full-time faculty and staff. I was somewhat surprised as I always viewed these positions as interchangeable in scope, but that was not to be the case here at Keene. This announcement put a damper on my future at Keene since I definitely needed a full-time position. Ruth, as I stated, was keeping us afloat and I must mention here that I can only thank her for sticking with me as I tried to fulfill my dream. After ruminating over the decision of the college and getting tired of traveling, it started to take its toll. The situation wasn't coming together as I had planned. We were even considering looking at buying a home in the area, but it just wasn't going to be.

I felt myself starting to become disorganized in my coaching, along with a sense of hopelessness that was leading me to yet another mood swing. I again was on the verge of dealing with depression and all that goes with it. It didn't take much and I guess the uncertainty of my family's future was starting to overwhelm me. I began to talk to Ruth about my overall outlook. She again supported me and told me to try to deal with it one day at a time.

One day during an indoor practice I stood in the middle of the field house and became mentally paralyzed. I couldn't follow my workout schedule at all so I dismissed the team until the next day. Well the next day never arrived as I got into my car and headed home. I needed help and I knew it. Since the last episode of this kind, I hadn't been going to therapy on a regular basis. I did have a doctor that I did go to occasionally so I made an appointment to see him. I also informed the athletic director at Keene that I was taking a leave from the position. There was an assistant who would be able to assume the practices until I returned. Of course the reasoning was somewhat of a fabrication as I wasn't sick in a physical sense, but was rather dealing with that demon again. I also wasn't comfortable exposing any more details. When you deal with this malady, you pick your spots; hopefully mentioning it to people you think will be good listeners and show some understanding. Sometimes this isn't the way it works out, and you have to deal with people who have different responses.

Things didn't get any better, I wasn't on medications, and finally I thought I needed a rest. So the doctor and I decided that perhaps hospitalization would help me through this. Ruth agreed and I entered a hospital in February. This hospital was located in New Hampshire and we hoped that it could afford me professional support on a daily basis. The hospital was primarily caring for alcoholics but some of the programs had some overlap. It was kind of interesting that during my stay there I saw much similarity between my affliction and theirs'. In fact they had a 'double whammy' in that they also were depressed due to their alcohol abuse. Making this decision seemed to calm me down, but that was short lived. The experience of entering an institution of this kind that deals primarily with people with substance abuse problems is a whole different ballgame. You are already looked at as not having control of your life so they issue stringent rules and regulations. This part of this book was perhaps the most difficult to reduce to writing, but it had to be told as it was a life event that I went through and in the final analysis, coaching baseball played an important part.

After the hospital stay, I was fortunate to again return to help Ted out with the UNH team as a second assistant coach. I was just helping out when needed. All I remember about coming back is that when I boarded the team bus wearing a different uniform that didn't fit well, (baseball players have a thing about uniforms fitting just right) I felt uncomfortable. But I was back on the bus again, going to Providence College, to be part of baseball again. I was very nervous as I didn't yet feel part of the team, but was just along for the ride. As we were taking our pre-game warm up, I went to Ted and asked him if I could throw batting practice. He said, "Sure", and I went out to the mound behind the protective screen. I hadn't thrown a ball since late October, but I knew this is what I had to do. You have thirty minutes to complete this ritual so you go through all the position players, and then give a quick round to the starting lineup. You need to have control and throw strikes. At first I was all over the place, but finally, everything clicked in and I was back where I wanted to be, on a baseball field dealing with young adults. I can honestly say that as I was toweling myself down after BP, I started to feel that balance I needed in my life return to me. Baseball always gave me the feeling of being at home and doing something that I had a passion for. That season was not a great one for UNH. We finished around .500 and didn't make the playoffs. But for me it was very special and so needed.

During that May I was getting ready to take the comprehensive exams for my Master's Degree in Counseling. I had been studying and completing course work that I had not worked on for a while as I was given an extension due to my hospital stay. I took the exam by myself under the direction of my professor who was also my advisor. The test consisted of six questions dealing with all aspects of counseling, with each question being allotted one hour. There were three questions in the morning, a lunch break, and the final three in the afternoon. My advisor gave me the first three and told me to go to a classroom next to his office and begin the exam. He also informed me that he would be in and out as he had errands to do. So when I finished I was to put the test in a manila folder on his desk. I then went to lunch and returned to finish the exam. Again, I was given an envelope with three questions in it. I went to the classroom, took a deep breath, and opened the envelope. When you take an exam of this length on subject matter that is somewhat intertwined, you sometimes feel that in answering the questions you overlap your points of reference and begin to repeat yourself. As I looked at these questions I immediately knew that they read like the questions I had been given in the morning! In fact they were!! Someone had collated them incorrectly. I immediately went next door to my professor's office, but he was nowhere to be found and since this was a Saturday there was no one else around to assist me. I called his home but to no avail, so I decided to go home and wait a while to call him again. I did and he answered. Upon hearing my predicament he told me to meet him at his office and he would find the right questions. When I returned to his office, he knew that I was somewhat frazzled so he told me to go home and finish the rest of the exam and return it on Monday. So here I was completing my comprehensive exam at home on my kitchen table. You might think that this was a great advantage, a take-home final; however, being at home wasn't the best testing atmosphere and I had all I could do to get my mind back on the exam questions. I decided not to wait until I was better focused, like waiting until Sunday. I just knew I had to complete the exam on the day I was assigned to take it. So I answered the last three questions, took them back to his office, and slid them under his office door. A week later I found out that I had passed and would receive my diploma. What an experience, definitely one I would never forget!

CHAPTER 11 TRIVIA QUESTION

What team started uniform numbering?

CHAPTER 12
CAREER CHANGE

Since I was not yet gainfully employed I began looking for a school counselor's job in the area. It was the end of the school year and not too many positions were available. My hope was that sometime during the summer, a position would become available when someone contemplating retirement would do so and allow me to compete for a position. The summer moved along and I wasn't interviewing much. One Sunday I noticed an opening for a Director of Guidance at a high school in the Lakes Region. I immediately inquired about it, but had not given it much thought because it was an administrative position. I didn't think I was ready for yet another administrator's job. I just wanted a school counselor's position dealing directly with students, but the summer was flying by, so I filled out the appropriate paper work and applied. I received a phone call the next week and was told that my interview would be at 7 a.m. in the morning. This was the earliest I'd ever been asked to sell myself to anyone. The school district was about an hour north of Durham so I left early to be there with some time to spare.

Upon entering the high school, I was greeted by the principal's secretary, who also was an early riser. She told me that the principal was going to be a little late, but I would be seeing the guidance secretary first since as she gleefully put it, "That's who you will be really working for." We hit it off immediately and as we were conversing I ran into a complicated matter of sorts. As I was adjusting myself in the chair, I noticed that my pants zipper had come apart! I nervously tried to fix it, but to no avail. At this point the secretary reentered the room and I was up front with her (no pun intended) and told her of my dilemma. She tossed me a Program of Studies booklet and told me to put it on my lap. In a few minutes the principal entered and I stood up very cautiously to greet him with the Program of Studies strategically positioned. He, of course, was unaware of my predicament. We talked and I answered a myriad of questions concerning the position at which time he stated that the Superintendent of Schools was coming in and he would like me to meet him. He told me to look over the office area and to ask any additional questions I had of the secretary. As he was about to leave, the secretary whose name was Alexis told him that he had just interviewed Mr. Michel with his fly open. The principal broke out into hysterics as I removed the Program of Studies from my lap. He then stated that he was impressed with me from the onset of the interview in that I was the first candidate that he had spoken with who had taken the time to review the Program of Studies to see what type of syllabus was being offered at the high school. The Superintendent was also made privy of my situation and I got the job "hands down" or should I say, "fly down". Incidents like this one are sometimes meant to be. During this whole event I got to know the tenor of the people I would be working with and this proved to be true throughout my tenure at this school.

I continued to coach at UNH on a part time basis, returning every afternoon to Durham for practice. I was full time on the weekends and I had arranged with the school to be able to use some of my vacation time toward going south with the team during the

March break. This arrangement was made possible by the Superintendent who viewed my position as administrative and said, "Pete, you are being hired for 210 days a year, you decide how to use your time and get the best results." He was a down-to-earth person who treated his subordinates very professionally. Of course, the principal had to deal with this somewhat touchy situation when he was asked by the faculty why I was given this preferential treatment. He handled it with much aplomb and in a professional manner. I met all my yearly goals, but I must admit when I came back with a tan, I know I 'ticked' some people off.

During the early 90s rumors started to surface that the administration at UNH was reviewing all their athletic programs to see if they could do any restructuring to reduce their budget cost. We had heard this before especially in relation to spring sports. Coaching athletics in the spring in New England as I stated before has it minuses. The weather always plays havoc with scheduling, and the season is so brief that you sometimes have difficulty in completing the league schedule. Baseball above all was affected by this the most. Time was always of the essence and with the school year ending the first week of May, you had about six weeks of actual playing time. Unlike a sport like lacrosse, we couldn't compete in extremely foul weather so we had to postpone and reschedule games throughout the season. We did compete sometimes in less than perfect conditions, which I always thought was detrimental to the sport in that athletes were asked to perform under conditions that didn't allow them to execute properly. We continued coaching with this shroud hanging over us. It started to become an issue in recruiting as the word was out that UNH might possibly be considering eliminating its baseball program. Remember in the State University System this had already been done at Keene State so a precedent of sorts had been established.

Baseball in the Northeast in most cases is not a revenue producing sport. Usually you don't charge admission to games so all you might do is pass the hat around a grandstand in the seventh inning or sell T-shirts behind the backstop. Sometimes you might institute a 50/50 drawing if you expect a decent crowd. This is one of the criteria that would be brought to the committee whose charge would be to review the athletic programs. So you get the picture. I guess to use baseball parlance, we had three strikes against us; weather, short season, and a non-revenue producing sport. An additional criterion that also entered the decision making process was that of Title IX compliance. Remember my dealing with it as a public school athletic director in the early 70's? The same issues prevailed and had to be deliberated upon.

The head coach had been at the helm for over twenty-five years, teaching and coaching baseball. I say teaching in that he had a very popular baseball coaching course that was well received not only by the undergrads, but by people in the community who were becoming interested in coaching youth sports. He decided to retire after the 1993 season and I had to, at that time, make a personal decision. Did I want to apply for the head job? I think at this point you the reader already know the answer - absolutely! I went ahead and got my resume ready for the interview process. I was keenly aware that this program due to his retirement was going to have some changes. I applied for the position, was granted an interview, and did not become the successful candidate. So at this point I decided I had been an assistant long enough, and I submitted my resignation. The intercollegiate baseball program lasted another four years, when in the spring of 1997 it played its last games. The committee that was assigned to review the athletic program recommended that men's baseball, men's lacrosse, and men's and women's golf be eliminated. The recommendations were accepted and agreed upon by those who had issued the charge. You can imagine the fury that this decision caused.

A groundswell of support to have baseball reinstated immediately surfaced. An initial meeting was held on campus which was attended by approximately two hundred people: alumni, former players, parents of current players, and fans who turned out to voice their disapproval. If you were an underclassman on the team, you now were put in the unenviable position of deciding whether or not to transfer to another school to continue your education and play baseball. If you had any scholarship money, the question was, would the scholarship money continue for your schooling without baseball? The underlying factor from my perspective was that many athletes had already declared their majors and a transfer seemed unfavorable.

Like most initial meetings over an unfavorable decision, many people turned out. But as it played out, only a few people continued to carry the torch to see if they could reverse this decision. Other meetings were scheduled, and all options were discussed, legal or otherwise. In the final analysis, the die was cast and the national pastime at UNH became history after over one hundred years in existence.

Initially, I attended some of the meetings that a group formed to try to reinstate the baseball program. This group secured the services of the legal profession. A lawyer in the area, who was a baseball fan and in fact was still playing in an adult league, was hired to assist us. Mentioning his playing in this league is another spin off of this great game, senior participation. But that's a story for another time.

After a few meetings, papers were put into place to consider some type of legal action based on the Title IX mandate that the University had made in some of its original decision making. This action of reducing athletic programs at the college level was not only happening at UNH, but was also happening around the nation. So we were in contact with other interested parties who were trying to gather information perhaps to take it to the highest court in the land. In doing this, the goal was to have a landmark decision made in our favor. I was not privy to all the litigation procedures, but it mainly dealt with the fact that men's athletics was being affected in an adverse way by the interpretation being followed as it related to the federal law. Unfortunately to go through all of these legal proceedings required money and there was not the resources to go to this level as it would have been prohibitive in cost. After reviewing all the facts, the attorneys had concluded that there wasn't much of a chance to come away with a favorable decision. So, again, things simmered down and the spring season at UNH consisted of men's track and field, and men's and women's tennis.

CHAPTER 12 TRIVIA QUESTION

How did the bleachers get their name?

CHAPTER 13
UNH CLUB BASEBALL

In December of 1999 I was sitting in my high school guidance office when a young lady, who knew I was a baseball fan, came into my office announcing that baseball was returning to UNH as a club sport. A friend of hers had seen signs posted around the campus about an organizational meeting. This friend was a freshman who was dating a young man who was still a senior at this high school who played baseball on the varsity team. He was interested in going to UNH and she had faxed him a copy of the meeting announcement. After receiving a copy of this, I called down to the campus recreation department and spoke directly to the Sports Club Director. She filled me in on the particulars and I told her that I would be interested in helping out. She was aware of my previous coaching at UNH, and asked me to attend the meeting.

The meeting was held just before Christmas break and was attended by over one hundred interested candidates. The number surprised me somewhat, but after those in attendance heard what the commitment was going to be, the number decreased to seventy-five. The next meeting to be held was in January, 2000. Two students were responsible for this interest in club baseball. One was a graduate who had assisted the varsity program in its final years. The other was a sophomore who had the energy and passion to pursue this undertaking. Initially when you are a first-time club, the Campus Recreation Department does not provide you with any funding so you are on your own until you prove that the club is a viable organization, with dues paying members, officers, and a constitution. From my point of view this was the start of something special, and what has transpired since has become very rewarding for all who continue to be involved, especially the new head coach. You see on Christmas Eve day I had received a phone call from the young graduate coach stating that he had been offered an assistant's position at Dartmouth College. His concern was that he was going to leave a group of enthusiastic men in the lurch, and he wanted some advice as to how to break this news to them. I offered some suggestions and told him that I would assume the position providing that the students were in agreement. He thought that this would work out and I had the January meeting. As stated before, there was still a large amount of interest and to attempt to pick a team that would be manageable to coach and also provide a worthwhile experience for the student athletes became my first task.

So from the get-go our club assumed a different status in that we decided to have tryouts. This was to be serious baseball! It took a lot of organization to hold tryouts that gave the students the feeling that they were given a fair assessment of their talent. Of course, all this had to be conducted indoors on the third floor of the recreation center which was a large 3-court basketball area. We did what I thought was a good job in determining who would become club members and we decided to keep a roster of thirty-five players. Again, this was a large number, but we would rotate players on each weekend when we played games. By doing this we stayed within the philosophy of sport clubs, which is having as many students as possible involved. We scheduled some prep school and community tech colleges. Our first contest in fact was against Phillips Exeter Academy on Saturday, April 1, at their field. We had a beautiful day to play and although the outcome was not in our favor, we were just happy to be playing baseball again. A side note is that we lost by a score of 8-7, only to be beaten by a young man who for many years was the UNH bat boy when Ted and I were coaching. This young man has continued his baseball successes and by the time this book is completed, I feel confident that he will make the 'big time'.

It was an eclectic group of opponents, but in the spring of 2000, UNH baseball was back in business and representing the university again. This team had about five players who were freshmen on the last intercollegiate team in 1997 so they immediately were charter members. In looking back it gave me much pleasure and pride to have seen these young men playing baseball again for their college. This was to be worth all the hassle that came with starting a club team, especially since there was still hard feelings evident dealing with the demise of the intercollegiate team. But we prevailed and selected the officers for the coming year, adopted a club constitution, and my responsibility was to come up with the fall schedule.

We also took on an ambitious project of going to Florida for a spring training trip. As a club team, this is a large undertaking, both financially and logistically, but since the year 2002 we have managed to accomplish this, going every other year. We have also received alumni support, namely the UNH Florida Southwest Chapter. They have provided us with a reception and cookout at our last game before we head north. This experience, student athlete meeting with alumni has been very rewarding for all involved. Hopefully, this event will continue each time we make the trip to Florida.

On our last trip, which was in the spring of 2006, we had two experiences that need to be told! We played in a tournament in Port Charlotte and stayed in a motel in town twenty minutes away, Englewood. After one morning game, we stopped off at a Wendy's for lunch. Here we met a group of older gentlemen who had just finished playing in the over sixty-five softball league. One of the players was a resident of Englewood who happened to have a grapefruit grove. He asked if we would be interested in having fresh grapefruit for breakfast. We said we would welcome this offer. So for the next three mornings, grapefruits were delivered for our consumption. At least for those mornings, the players had a healthy beginning to their day,

The second experience was somewhat unnerving, as you will see. When you travel by air, especially nowadays, planning your departure is very important. One needs lead time and everything must go like clockwork. Well, we started our trip home at five in the morning as we wanted to have sufficient time to arrive at the Tampa Airport for a 7:40 departure.

As we were riding north on the same route we had traveled eight days earlier, I turned to my assistant, Bob, and asked him when will we come to that long expansion bridge across Tampa Bay, the same one we traveled over on the way down? He said that it was coming up, but after checking the map, we discovered that we had indeed missed a turnoff exit and were heading north going on the east side of Tampa! We gathered ourselves, looked at our watches, and began to look for a highway that would take us west back to the airport. Having done this successfully, however, we had to go directly through downtown Tampa.

So here it is, six o'clock in the morning and still not comfortable with our surroundings. So much so that I stopped and went across the road to a breakfast place to ask for directions. Upon entering, I noticed a female police officer having a cup of coffee and I proceeded to ask for the quickest way to the Tampa Airport. She looked at me and replied, "I'll tell you as soon as you park your vans correctly!" You see, we were 'live' parking in a restricted area and she was adamant that we park where we should. I couldn't believe it, but yelled to my assistant to bring the vans over to park them correctly. This definitely cut into our time schedule.

With directions in hand, we proceeded to the toll booth. We asked for the exit number that would take us back to the airport. Unfortunately, the toll collector did not speak English, so using my Spanish taken many, many years ago, I was able to understand, "exit eight", and off we went. As we drove by exit one through seven, we then came upon exit nine!!! Where was exit eight? Just as we were about to pull off and accept that we were not going to make our plane, exit eight appeared! Don't ask me to explain this because I cannot, but we got to the airport car rental area, then to the tram that takes you to the terminal and started to check our personal baggage along with seven bags of team gear, only to hear the person in charge say, "You have a slim chance of making the flight." That's just what I wanted to hear! I said, "We are going to give it our best shot." Miraculously, we made it, running with shoes in hand, as we boarded the plane. Over the plane's intercom, we heard, "Welcome University of New Hampshire Baseball Team." I always tell my guys, "Expect the unexpected".

CHAPTER 13 TRIVIA QUESTION

What was the name of the one time Brooklyn

Dodger bat boy?

CHAPTER 14
HELL'S HALF ACRE

Things have a way of working out and this experience in my life couldn't have come at a better time. I was contemplating retirement, and this would be, and was, a natural transition for me. The time was right and I was retiring after almost forty years in the education field in one capacity or another. As the assistant coach at UNH early on, I made many contacts with many coaches in the area, so obtaining games for the fall season proved to be no problem. However, finding a field to practice and play games on was another matter. After much searching, I was able to secure what was called the outer field on the UNH athletic practice grounds. Not only was it far away from the campus, but it was located in the lowest area so drainage was something that had to be dealt with. This area was no more than a cow pasture, where we measured off base lines, threw down bases, and played. No mound, just a surface with many undulations. Fielding ground balls became a challenge, and we started calling the area 'hell's half acre'. If it rained just a little, the field would be unplayable and practice was curtailed. However, that fall it didn't rain much so we were lucky. The grass had to be mowed once a week so the players got their conditioning in by lining up on one foul line and they would proceed to mow the area with a push mower. To make it interesting, I took off the self-propelled attachment so the guys really got their legs and arms in shape. Necessity knows no law so we accepted this as a unique ritual. We practiced two to three days a week accomplishing a lot and we were prepared to play every weekend in the fall. I was able to secure the use of a local high school field to allow us to play our home games. The season lasted about six weeks, with approximately twenty games against Division II and III NCAA teams. These colleges used these games to select new players for their upcoming spring competition.

One tradition that was established at outer field was a game entitled 'Fungo Golf'. Since we practiced next to a practice football field which had goal posts at each end, we devised a game that was introduced by one of my assistants, Steve, who when playing pro ball, did this. You simply went to one end of the field and selected a goal post upright at the other end to be used as a golf flag. The person closest to the goal post would be declared the winner. We alternated each end and had one fun time. Hitting a fungo in itself is an art, but to try to place it a hundred yards away was very challenging. On my first try ever, I had what could be considered a 'hole in one' in Fungo Golf as I hit a fungo and saw my ball roll directly to the base of the goal post upright. I have a picture to prove it! The coaches did this while the players began practice with what we call 'everydays' which amounted to one lap around 'hell's half acre', stretching, and playing catch. Sometimes the players joined us prior or after practice to play the game. This was good fun and added a different dimension to the practice. We used this facility for three seasons and it became our 'field of dreams'. We even convinced the UNH ground's crew to cut the grass and put down foul lines and a batter's box. We eventually moved to a synthetic playing surface area that has afforded us better playing conditions.

After playing in the spring of 2000 and the fall of the same year, some of my players asked if we could perhaps form a league of some kind so we would have a goal to strive for, namely a club baseball championship. I went about investigating the possibility knowing that there were some colleges that had club baseball programs. My first inquiry was with Boston University who had ended their intercollegiate program a few years before UNH. They seemed interested and said that they would meet with their Sport Club Director to see if a program could be started. I also contacted some smaller schools in Maine who played baseball in the fall. Two teams were interested so we had a meeting at one of the Maine schools and formed the New England Club Baseball Association (NECBA). The first year we had a six game schedule but it has grown so we now have five teams and play a twelve game schedule with a double elimination playoff at the end, hosted at different sites each year. The teams that are in the league presently are: Boston University, University of New England, Central Maine Community College, University of Maine, and UNH. At this time we are looking again to add more teams. We would like to have a few more community colleges join us, the format being a northern and southern division. This would cut down on transportation costs as we would play within each division and have a crossover game with the other division. We would end the season with the southern division champ playing the northern division champ at a neutral site.

We have already had great success and recently opened our 2003 season with a showcase tournament at Mansfield Stadium in Bangor, Maine. This field is a first class venue and was donated to the town of Bangor by Stephen King who is himself an avid baseball fan. In fact, he has a home behind the outfield fence, but far enough away that it is unreachable with a home run shot. We were very fortunate to have this facility to use and are grateful to all that made it possible.

This baseball experience has been truly the highlight of my coaching career. Being around young athletes who truly play for the love of the game makes it that much more rewarding. Personally this is not an end for me, but rather a beginning. I am always aware of the fact that I will have some down times, which is part of my being, but baseball continues to be the vehicle for the balance that I need in my life. It goes without saying that this prompted me to reduce all of my feeling to writing this book. I had to do this because I sincerely believe that many of us need something to enjoy that is not related to a pay check. I have gotten this enjoyment and am thankful for it.

However, this is still an ongoing project not without glitches and disappointments. The disappointments are not always scoreboard related. In dealing with young adults who are still maturing and looking for direction, I find that many lack certain attributes that would help them in their life's journey some of which are lack of time management, punctuality, and commitment. Yes, they are in college so they are experiencing a different lifestyle and independence, but they often need guidance and someone to tell them about the 'real' world. It is all right to be somewhat laid back during this time of one's life, but to be unaware of commitments that are expected, and the responsibility therein, leads to confusion when it comes to living in an orderly fashion. I feel being involved in any extracurricular activity lends itself to having that structure that we all need some more than others. We need a base on which to fall back when things become overwhelming as growing nowadays is not easy. Notice, I didn't say "growing up". You never do. Everyone grows each and every day. As my grandma once told my parents, "Don't ever take the boy out of him".

I hope that through my coaching and listening, I have given my players a chance to focus, to have visions, and make goals for their adult years ahead of them.

CHAPTER 14 TRIVIA QUESTION;

Point to Ponder: Why is the foul pole not called a

fair pole?

CHAPTER 15
MY THOUGHTS ON
BASEBALL'S FUTURE

The future for baseball as the national fabric that allows all populations to come together and enjoy the same experience is alive and well. For a period of time, at the end of the twentieth century, baseball in general was being viewed in an unfavorable light. The economics of the business (and it is a business) had gotten out of control with spiraling costs brought about by enormous salaries that were given to players by owners who wanted their business to have the best product. Avarice and greed go hand in hand, and this was becoming very evident as the local fan was being asked to support this with increased ticket prices.

Baseball became for me an old friend that had to be revisited. I personally believe that as we begin the twenty-first century, baseball is beginning to look at itself, trying to deal with those factors that were alienating its fans. In this age we must accept that baseball and in fact all professional sports, are entertainment and we will pay for it if it gives us a good performance. This is where baseball has left itself vulnerable to criticism. The caliber of play has become watered down with too many young players being rushed into the major leagues without the proper preparation at the minor league level.

The whole infrastructure of baseball, as we used to know it, has been compacted. We now have only three levels of minor league play and the rookie instructional short season leagues. Players can move up rapidly to major league status much faster than in the past. Expanding to more major league teams would be detrimental at this point in time. Presently, baseball is considering cutting back in certain regions where the cities cannot afford to support a team. This is a good sign and I feel it will bode well for the preservation of baseball.

Another area of concern is the area of escalating salaries, agents, and collective bargaining. Baseball as entertainment is a business being run by professionals who want to earn a profit. Labor negotiations in our country have been on going since the beginning of our national work force existence. How we actually conduct the interaction between owner and worker is the key to future successes. We can ill afford to have any more walk-outs, canceling of seasons and World Series. Currently there have been signs of compromise on each side and this is healthy for baseball. Its popularity is again at its zenith, but we must be ever vigilant that there is a balance between those two factions.

Baseball is Americana. We don't have to dispute whether in fact it was actually founded in this country. It is here and it has a strong rooted foundation with faithful followers. Its impact on society is evident. One only has to attend a game, sit with strangers, and find oneself passing hot dogs along and giving high fives as your team rallies. The bonding is instant once you root for the 'old ball team'.

LAST TRIVIA QUESTION

What does the saying "Can of Corn" signify in

baseball, and how did the phrase originate?

EPILOGUE

This narrative reflects my professional and private feelings like threads in a baseball, intertwined yet somehow coming out whole. My hope is that you too can find something in your lives to help you overcome the many stresses of everyday living and, ultimately, to see that the 'joy is in the struggle'.

Finally, what does the saying 'Can of Corn' signify in baseball, and how did it originate?

A Can of Corn in baseball signifies an outfielder catching a fly ball. It originated when entering a grocery store, asking for a can of corn, the grocer would take a pole with pinchers attached to it and reach to the top shelf of the canned vegetable area, grab the can, and then release it, having it fall into his hands. This simple task of catching the can of corn became a saying for a lazy fly ball.

Yours in baseball.

Pete Michel

TRIVIA ANSWERS

Chapter 1 Answer: They were given the name "Dodgers" due to the fact that when the spectators were going to the game they had to 'dodge* the trolley cars to get to the ball field.

Chapter 2 Answer: Originally the pitching position was in a box where the pitcher could run from the back to the front of the designated box before releasing his pitch.

Chapter 3 Answer: At one time there were eleven players in the field. The three infielders actually stayed at their bases and two players stood on either side of the pitcher. These players were known as the 'short stops'.

Chapter 4 Answer: The area of the field behind the outfield got its name from a Bull Durham cigarette sign which was located behind the fence at an old ballpark

Chapter 5 Answer: Players would be allowed to toss their gloves on the field as they left their positions to hit.

Chapter 6 Answer: It was known as "Coogan's Bluff".

Chapter 7 Answer: It was a circle.

Chapter 8 Answer: 'Leading-off', 'on deck' and 'in the hold'.

Chapter 9 Answer: Pitcher Sal Maglie.

Chapter 10 Answer: The Newlyweds.

Chapter 11 Answer: The New York Yankees

Chapter 12 Answer: The wooden boards got bleached by the sun.

Chapter 13 Answer: Charlie DiGovanni

Chapter 14 Answer: No answer!!

Printed in the United States
89349LV00001B/103-198/A